FOUR WARNINGS

Before The End Times Begin

A Literal (Non-Hype) Perspective

By: David Brennan

FOUR WARNINGS BEFORE THE END TIMES BEGIN

Website for this book: TrueProphecyNews.com

ISBN: 978-0-9887614-6-9

Retailers and distributors qualify for special discounts on bulk purchases. For more information, email True Prophecy News at:

TrueProphecyNews@Gmail.com

Contents

Introduction

The unfortunate reality associated with many Bible prophecy "experts" and "scholars" is the degree to which they apply different interpretations to the same prophetic passages, often arriving at dramatically different conclusions. The "experts" who appear to do this the most are those who take a less literal view of the holy verses. Such an approach naturally results in a great degree of latitude for the interpreter to impart their version of what the holy words are saying. The main culprit here is viewing the multitude of direct and straightforward verses of prophetic Scripture from a non-literal perspective. The result of this non-literal approach is that the "interpreter" is able to plug in different meanings into the verse that satisfy their own standards which can vary greatly based on who is doing the interpreting. Often this is done in order to enable a verse to fit within some overall prophetic thesis, with the end result presented with a very personal perspective. This is not to say that there are not passages of prophetic Scripture that rely heavily on symbolism, which can easily produce a difference of opinions on their meanings. Such verses are to be found especially in the Books of Daniel and Revelation. For example, in the Book of Revelation, chapter 6, the different colors of the Four Horsemen of the Apocalypse have created an array of interpretations to be applied to each horse based simply on those colors.

We are told in the Scriptures that the Lord is a God of order and not confusion. Since the non-literal, liberal or figurative method of reading prophetic verses creates so much latitude in its interpretation, and frequently almost as many interpretations as there are individuals applying it, it is doubtful that such an approach which breeds so much confusion is approved by God. Also, this loose or non-literal approach to the prophetic Scriptures does not speak to the glory of God but to the glory of the individuals who are doing the interpreting. They suddenly become critical for understanding Scripture because it was they who found the correct meaning ... at least in their opinion. But because God says exactly what He means and means exactly what He says, He does not need man to plug in his own personal interpretations.

This book applies a very literal reading to an array of prophetic Scriptures to eliminate, as much as possible, the influence of personal interpretations. When, for example, in Matthew 24:6 we are told by Jesus concerning certain events described in the verse that *"the end is not yet,"* it is taken to mean literally that. However, in the next verse, Matthew 24:7, the events contained within it are described as being the *"beginning of sorrows"* and, again, it is taken here to mean exactly that ... the beginning of the end times. As such, it is accepted that verse 6 and verse 7 are describing two separate prophetic time frames that are placed immediately next to each other for good reason. The events in verse 6 are a rendition of what occurs just before the end times begin, whereas the events in verse 7 mark the actual start of the end times. Although this is literally what these two verses are indicating, many "experts" blend both verses into a single event and prophetic time frame. This book will not do that but reads them as literally as possible.

Another example of the approach taken here is that when, for instance, in Jeremiah 30 we see no sign of warfare against Israel, but *all nations devour, spoil,* and *prey* upon her, it is accepted this was not accomplished by warfare. When we see in Matthew 24:7 that the birth pangs term "odin" (Greek) is used in Jesus' words, *"All these are the beginning of sorrows,"* we accept that it was literally placed there for the Divine reason of associating *"the beginning"* of the end times with the concept of birth pangs.

The second method employed here is the use of logical inference in association with literal interpretation. For example, when in Matthew 24:7 we are told *"Nation shall rise against nation and kingdom against kingdom,"* the fact it is indicated they must *"rise"* tells us they were not already in a state of war prior to the beginning of that verse. It is the literal reading of the verse that causes that logical conclusion. Also, because only nations and kingdoms are mentioned in the verse, it is taken as a literal description of government entities being in a state of war and not conflict involving internal rebellions, revolutions, violent movements, or civil wars. As a result of taking this approach, the broad license granted to those relying heavily on a loose, non-literal, liberal, or figurative reading of the Scriptures that allows great latitude to "interpret" is replaced here with the Scriptures being allowed to literally speak for themselves. Again, it is assumed God meant to say it exactly as He did.

In addition to taking a very literal approach, this effort also limits its scope to events occurring just prior to the launch of the end times as well as the events that constitute its beginning. The reason for doing this is to avoid the confusion that often sets in when mixing together the full spectrum of prophetic events across the entire span of the end times. If a person can establish a foundational understanding of what happens just prior to the beginning of the end times, as well as the events that constitute its actual beginning, then understanding the remaining events will flow naturally from there. In other words, this book seeks to establish a foundation.

Also this book does not rely on just a few verses to support its suppositions but considers what a multitude of verses say on the specific topics being addressed. It also requires at least two Scriptures to confirm each position taken. As a result, it uses literal Scriptural readings as confirmation of other literal Scriptural readings. The Biblical prophetical books, chapters, and verses that interlock to create the flow of events indicated here are these: *Matthew 24:4-8, 24; Luke 21:11-12, 24-25; 1 Thessalonians 5:1-3; Zechariah 14; Jeremiah 30; Joel 2:30-32, 3:1-2; Isaiah 10:5, 13:4-5,8,14, 14:13-14 34,2,8; Daniel 7:25-27, 9:24-27, 11:36, 12:77; Zephaniah 1:16 & 18; Revelation 6:1-12, 11:2-3, 17:12-13, 19:11-15;, and 2 Thessalonians 2:4.*

As can be seen, there is an array of Scriptural books and verses that come together to form the flow of events presented here.

God bless!

David Brennan

CHAPTER ONE

Matthew: Is an Israel-Iran War a Scriptural Necessity?

> **Covered in this Chapter:** Why Israel and Iran going to war may be necessary to complete Scripture before the end times can begin.
>
> **Covered in this Chapter:** Evidence that birth pang earthquakes and wars have not yet begun.

lthough the world would naturally see war between Israel and Iran as cause for great concern, very few would understand its Biblical significance. In fact, it will be presented that such a war resolving notable *rumours of wars* for restored Israel in association with *wonders in the heavens* would be one of the most ominous Biblical warnings possible for mankind. To begin understanding the Scriptural rendition supporting why such a war with heavenly signs represents a critical warning it is necessary to go back some 2,000 years to a hill located near Jerusalem. The year is approximately 32 A.D. and a Jewish Rabbi named Jesus has led his band of followers to a grove of olive trees just outside the city of Jerusalem. The trees are situated on a small hill referred to, appropriately, as the Mount of Olives. The words He is about to speak will shape the debates and opinions of Bible scholars for the next 2,000 years. In His discourse He will provide His curious apostles and future generations a technical breakdown of how to identify the specific events that will occur just before the launch of the feared end times.

Wars and Rumours of Wars

In the study of Bible prophecy we discover there are certain passages which become understandable only after a moment in history arrives. A good example of this is the various Scriptures describing the physical effects of a thermal nuclear detonation (Zech 14:12; Rev 8:7; Ezekiel 39:9, 14, 15; 2 Peter 3). It took "the bomb" in 1945 to fully appreciate those verses. And there is the case of Daniel the prophet who was told to *seal the book, even to the time of the end,* indicating that certain prophecies would be understandable only much later in time. Now it appears current history may have provided another epiphany moment of understanding.

The case is presented in this chapter that based on a literal reading of words spoken by Jesus on the Mount of Olives that current day Israel has to resolve notable *rumours of wars* before the flow of Bible prophecy can proceed. Based on that literal reading, combined with current geopolitical circumstances, that requirement could only be achieved by war between Israel and Iran. What flushed this detail out into the open is the constant war *rumours* between the two nations combined with a literal reading of the verses in question. Those *rumours of wars* have been as unique as they are persistent since the year 2002, when it became clear Iran was building a nuclear weapons program. Since that year most experts have agreed that such a war between Israel and Iran would immediately draw Israel into conflict with Hamas in Gaza, and Hezbollah in Lebanon, since both are proxy allies of Iran on Israel's borders. Therefore, since the year 2002, it has been *rumours of wars* in the plural sense specifically fulfilling the Scriptural warning in detail.

In considering the Scriptural case presented here, the reader will face two challenges. The first challenge is to allow the Scriptures to simply speak for themselves. This statement may sound simple, but often it is difficult to accept the literal meaning of a verse after having been told it really means something else. The second challenge is similar to the first and pertains to certain geopolitical and geological facts presented here. These facts dispute current teachings in certain prophecy circles today. But they are still hard and true facts. They are presented here in support of this thesis, as well as to begin the process of removing the confusion and error surrounding both.

The Scriptural Case

Of all the prophetic words spoken by Jesus during His ministry, it is the Olivet Discourse which provides the most detailed and sweeping rendition of the grand events popularly referred to as the end times. His talk begins after being asked by His disciples a very simple question. Their question comes just after Jesus startles them by describing how the massive Jewish Temple located in Jerusalem, the center of Jewish life in that day, would be destroyed to the point that not one stone would be left upon another. Naturally, after hearing of the impending fate of their precious temple, they not only ask Him when it will happen but, more significantly for current times, *what shall be the sign of thy coming, and of the end of the age?* It is His response to that question that Jesus begins providing a detailed explanation of end time events in what is referred to as the Olivet Discourse.

The approach He takes in answering such an important question is the one any thinking person would employ. He starts by describing the signs that will come just before the beginning of the end times. Then after describing those signs, He immediately details the actual beginning events. By taking this approach it allows Him to very specifically answer their question because He is able to clearly identify the precise moment it all begins. He completely fulfills their request in the spirit of *Ask, and it shall be given you; seek, and ye shall find; knock, and it shall be opened unto you.* They asked a specific question and then received a specific answer. By doing this, He provided future generations the exact signs that come just before it all launches. In fact, by reading His words literally He establishes a detailed warning system whose signs cannot be confused.

It is advised that you consider His words with great care and allow the Scriptures to tell you what He is saying by reading them very literally. The most notable confusion surrounding the next three verses is the belief they are speaking about a single vague beginning of the end times. But when reading them literally it is clear that He presents two distinct events within two different prophetic time frames, which allow a clear beginning moment to be identified. That concept is a key understanding. First, consider verse 6.

---

⁶And ye shall hear of wars and rumours of wars: see that ye be not troubled: for all these things must come to pass, but the end is not yet.

After reading this verse, several points become clear. The events being described are not part of the end times since Jesus states, quite matter-of-factly, *the end is not yet.* In line with that statement, He says *be not troubled.* Essentially He is saying that during a time of *wars and rumours of wars* to *be not troubled* because *the end is not yet.* By taking His words literally, there is no other conclusion possible but that the end times have not yet started in this verse. So we will classify the events within this verse as existing within the prophetic pre-birth pangs time frame since the end times have not yet begun. But notice that Jesus does not tell us who is involved in these *wars and rumours of wars.* He only tells a group of Israelites you *shall hear of them.* Now consider verses 7 and 8.

---

⁷ For nation shall rise against nation, and kingdom against kingdom: and there shall be famines, and pestilences, and earthquakes, in divers places.

> *⁸ All these are the beginning of sorrows.*

Here, too, several points become immediately clear. By taking Jesus' words literally, it is clear the events discussed in verse 7 mark the start of the end times. We know this because after describing a series of signs in verse 7, He then in verse 8 advises us: *All these are the beginning of sorrows.* Note the word used here for *beginning of sorrows* is "odin," Greek for birth pangs. So the beginning moment of the end times is described by Jesus as birth pangs.

> **CRITICAL CONCLUSION:** THE *WARS AND RUMOURS OF WARS* IN VERSE 6 ARE A SEPARATE EVENT AND IN A PROPHETIC TIME FRAME PRIOR TO THE NATIONS AND KINGDOMS RISING TO WAR IN VERSE 7.

> **CRITICAL CONCLUSION:** VERSE 7 IS THE LITERAL BEGINNING OF THE END TIMES.

> **CRITICAL CONCLUSION:** JESUS LABELS THE BEGINNING OF THE END TIMES AS BIRTH PANGS.

It is important to note that after describing the events which constitute the beginning of the end times, Jesus refers to them as "birth pangs." Jesus also makes it clear that this event involves the nations going to war against one another by saying *nation shall rise against nation, and kingdom against kingdom.* We also know this is the actual beginning moment of the end times since the nations will have to *rise* and, therefore, will not already be at war with one another before verse 7 begins. In other words, something happens which causes them to *rise,* inferring a suddenness to it all. The Greek word used here for *rise* is "egerio" meaning "to arouse, or cause to rise." The nations are suddenly roused to war.

> **CRITICAL CONCLUSION:** BASED ON A LITERAL READING OF JESUS' WORDS, THE END TIMES LAUNCH WITH A GREAT WAR WHEREIN NATIONS ACROSS THE EARTH *RISE* AGAINST ONE ANOTHER.

Notice the subtle difference in the warlike conditions described in verse 6 from those in verse 7. While in verse 6 Jesus does not mention who is involved in those *wars and rumours of wars* as He speaks to a group of Israelites. But in verse 7, He specifies the nations and kingdoms, of the world. Additionally, because He names both nations and kingdoms it appears the magnitude of the conflict is great since He covers the full spectrum of government entities. This sounds like another world war. But there is something else here that is even more informative.

In describing wars in verse 6 with His statement *wars and rumours of wars,* through logical deduction and a literal read, it becomes impossible that Jesus is referring to the nations at conflict in that verse. Why? Because the events in verse 6 take place prior to the events in verse 7, so if the nations are already at war in verse 6, then how can they *rise* when verse 7 begins? In order to *rise,* those multitudes of nations and kingdoms must NOT already be in a state of general warfare with each other. This appears to be why Jesus does not mention the nations in verse 6. But that observation begs the following question: Who then is involved in those *wars and rumours of wars* described in verse 6 if it is not the nations?

CRITICAL CONCLUSION: IT APPEARS VERSE 6 CANNOT BE REFERRING TO THE NATIONS EXPERIENCING THOSE *WARS.*

Since a literal reading allows us to logically deduct that verse 6 cannot be referring to the nations, and the Bible is Israel-centric, consider the condition of Israel since returning as a nation in 1948. It is Israel that has experienced 14 major *wars* since coming back into the land. That is a significant war about every five years! Additionally, the Jewish state has experienced countless minor conflicts lasting from hours to several days. From the standpoint of *wars,* Israel has been fulfilling that requirement perfectly. But what about the *rumours* part of the verse? For Matthew 24:6 to apply to Israel, she must be involved in some kind of notable war *rumours* as well.

As mentioned earlier, it is since 2002 that Israel has experienced *rumours of wars* the like of which is unique in the twentieth century. The possibility of an Israel-Iran war was speculated on countless times over the years, even bringing the Israeli prime minister before the U.N. and the U.S. Congress to drive home its possibility to the world. It was an intense rumor that has been bubbling for well over a decade! However, just as Israel is perfectly fulfilling verse 6, the nations across the globe are fulfilling the condition required in verse 7.

CRITICAL CONCLUSION: VERSE 6 IS REFERRING TO ISRAEL
AND VERSE 7 THE NATIONS.

The Condition of the Nations

Since the nations must literally *rise* when verse 7 and the end times begin, we have reasoned they must be relatively peaceful going into the start of that verse. Remember, it is nations and kingdoms Jesus literally tells us to consider here. We are not concerned with internal rebellions, revolutions, violent movements, or civil wars. Jesus tells us nations and kingdoms. Put another way, Jesus is describing government entities going to war against one another. So now the following question arises: Has nation-to-nation warfare increased, or decreased over the last several decades? According to this perspective it should be decreasing and thus setting the stage for the nations to *rise* when verse 7 begins.

The Great Decline of Nation versus Nation Warfare

In a series of academic studies focusing on the phenomenon of war, one thing is clear warfare between nations has been trending down since the end of World War II. In fact, one such study speculates that the current lack of warfare between nation-states might be at its lowest point since the year 1495![1] Those studies have led to articles with titles like, "Think Again: War...World Peace Could be Closer than you Think"[2] in the prestigious *Foreign Policy* magazine, and "War Really is Going Out of Style"[3] published in *The New York Times.* However, this new condition among the nations does not mean warfare between nations has completely stopped. But it is an indication that the trend in warfare between nation-states has been dramatically and even historically down. For our purposes what these studies are really saying is that the nations across the earth are finally positioned to *rise* when verse 7 begins. Notice this is taking place just as Israel has perfectly fulfilled verse 6 with its multitude of wars since 1948 and its deep involvement in notable *rumours of wars.* The following chart on warfare deaths since the year 1946 tells the story. This data was derived by the Peace Research Institute Organization.

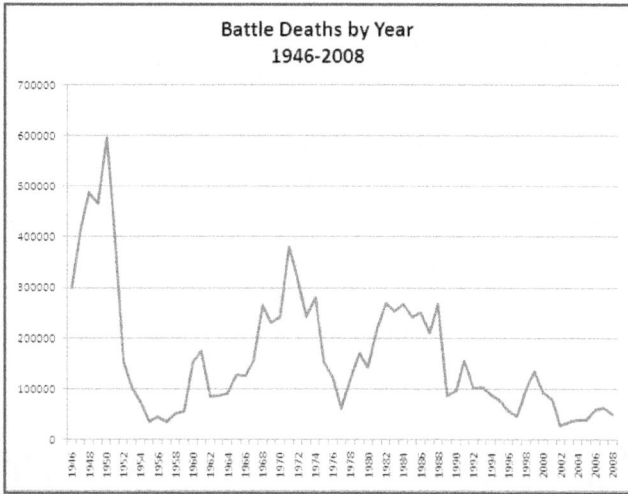

Battle Deaths by Year 1946-2008

http://www.politifact.com/punditfact/statements/2014/jul/21/stu-burguiere/fewer-wars-fewer-people-dying-wars-now-quite-some/

The Complete Lack of Scriptural Earthquake Activity

Further evidence verse 7 and the birth pangs of the end times have not yet begun is found in Jesus' warning that *earthquakes, in divers places* will accompany its beginning. As a result, when a significant earthquake strikes somewhere on earth, many claim it to be a prophetic birth pang. But that conclusion is simply not supported by geological facts. But before looking at those facts, consider the Scriptures associated with earthquakes.

Matthew 24:6-8.

6 And ye shall hear of wars and rumours of wars: see that ye be not troubled: for all these things must come to pass, but the end is not yet.

7 For nation shall rise against nation, and kingdom against kingdom: and there shall be famines, and pestilences, and earthquakes, in divers places.

8 All these are the beginning of sorrows.

Matthew tells us one of the signs that will accompany the start of the end times in verse 7 is that *earthquakes* will be taking place *in divers places*. The word used for *divers* is the Greek preposition "kata" which means "though out." So we are told earthquakes will be occurring throughout the world when the end times launch. But since earthquakes have been taking place throughout the Earth for thousands of years, this Scripture alone doesn't really help. All we know from it is that there will be earthquakes all over the earth. However, Luke 21:9-11 covers the same end time beginning events as Matthew 24:6-8 and we find an additional detail to the type of earthquakes that will be occurring all over the earth at the start of the end times. And this allows us to become much more precise in what to look for when it all begins.

> ⁹ But when ye shall hear of wars and commotions, be not terrified: for these things must first come to pass; but the end is not by and by.

> ¹⁰ Then said he unto them, Nation shall rise against nation, and kingdom against kingdom:

> ¹¹ And great earthquakes shall be in divers places, and famines, and pestilences; and fearful sights and great signs shall there be from heaven.

Here we are provided a significant qualifier that specifies the exact type of earthquakes we are to be looking for. We are told the earthquakes that will be all over the earth at the launch of the end times will be *great* ones. So to determine exactly what is meant by the term *great,* let's look at its meaning in the original Greek and what word in English best corresponds to it now.

The word used for *great* is the Greek adjective "megas" that produces the English word "mega" for something that is unusually large. So exactly what constitutes a "mega" earthquake? Consider what the United States Geological Survey (U.S.G.S.) says on the subject.

In an article published on April 17, 2016, after a series of earthquakes rocked Japan and Ecuador, the U.S.G.S. indicated there have been **no** "mega" earthquakes since seismic activity has been being measured over the last 100 years. And this statement was issued after earthquakes of 7.3 and 7.8 had just been recorded. The article and its link are located at the TrueProphecyNews.com website for your perusal.

The key understanding here is that this term "megas" is used to impart an exceptional nature to that which it is being applied. So the earthquakes associated with the birth pangs that launch the end times will be "mega" earthquakes. Although the U.S.G.S. indicates there have not been any "mega" earthquakes over the last 100 years, for the sake of the point being made here, consider the following graphs depicting earthquake activity going back to the year 1900. Although according to the U.S.G.S. the earthquakes depicted in these graphs are not considered "mega," they convey the indisputable point that even if the criteria for "mega" quakes is dramatically reduced, there is still no evidence to support that end times earthquake activity has begun yet.

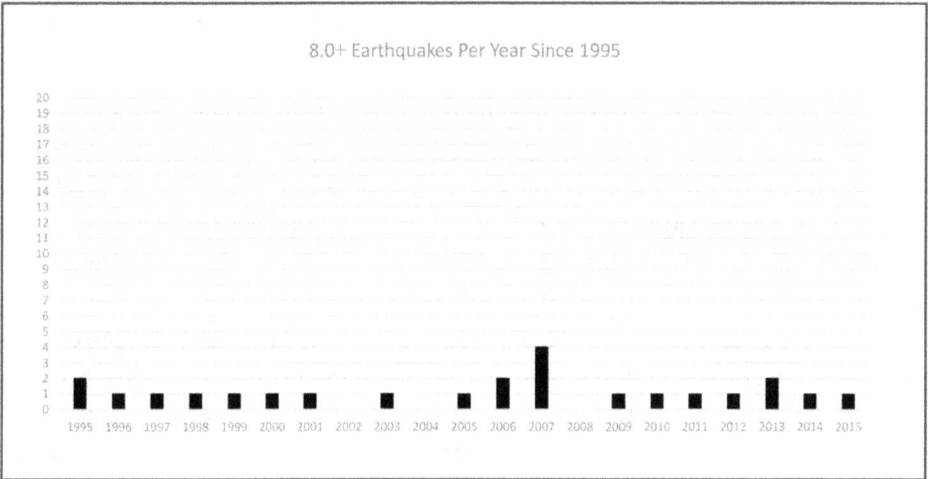

8.0+ Earthquakes Per Year Since 1995

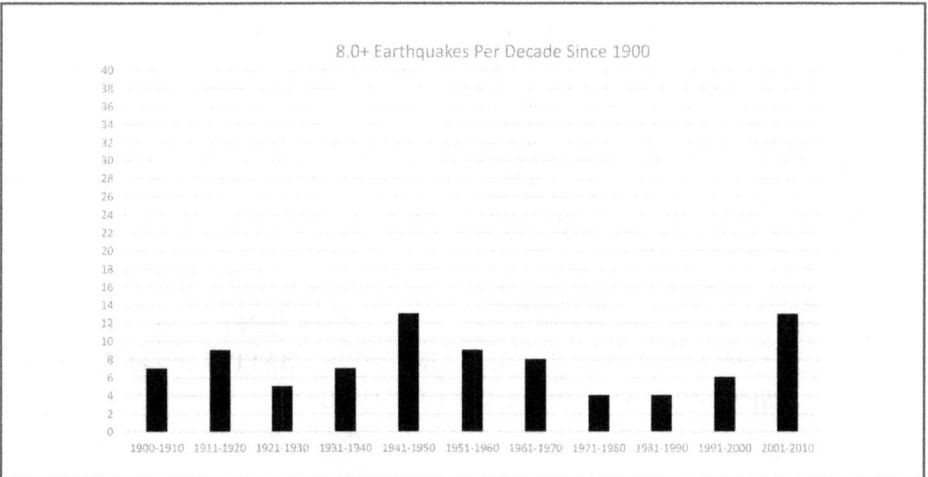

8.0+ Earthquakes Per Decade Since 1900

To verify these results simply go to the following link and you can plug in the criteria yourself. http://earthquake.usgs.gov/earthquakes/search/

Remember, the Scriptural requirement for earthquake activity that accompanies the start of end times birth pangs is *great* (mega) earthquakes all over the surface of the earth. Since this is what the Scriptures call for, and the above graphs are an accurate reflection of the lack of mega or great earthquakes across the earth, it is easy to reach a solid non-hyped conclusion: No... as of the year 2016, the birth pangs of the end times have absolutely not yet begun.

> CRITICAL CONCLUSION: MATTHEW 24:7 AND THE BIRTH PANGS OF THE END TIMES HAS NOT YET BEGUN AS OF APRIL 2016.

Conclusion

Our epiphany that verse 6 can only be referring to Israel makes it simple to then identify the nation embroiled in the Biblical *rumours of wars* with her. It is Iran but also included in those *rumours* is war with Hamas in Gaza and Hezbollah in Lebanon and thus equating to *rumours of wars* in the plural sense exactly as the Scripture calls for. This is because the war rumors between Israel and Iran have always included the rumor that it would include wars on Israel's northern border with Hezbollah and on its southern border with Hamas since both are proxy allies of Iran. Now a final question arises: What is the most realistic way verse 6 and its lengthy *rumours of wars* involving Israel can finally come to an end? This is an important question because the end of verse 6 will represent a significant geopolitical sign that the pre-birth pangs prophetic time frame is about to be completed. Since verse 6 is clearly in the pre-birth pangs time frame, then the birth pangs of the end times cannot launch in verse 7 until verse 6 is finished. If the above logic is correct, then there are only two ways verse 6 can end. One is if Israel and Iran come to peaceful terms, thus ending the *rumours of wars* for Israel. But that being highly unlikely leaves only one remaining way for it to complete. Israel and Iran must go to war to end the *rumours of wars* and finish verse 6, allowing the prophecies to proceed.

> CRITICAL CONCLUSION: A WAR BETWEEN ISRAEL AND IRAN APPEARS TO BE THE MOST LIKELY WAY MATTHEW 24:6 AND ITS *RUMOURS OF WARS* CAN BE RESOLVED.

What ultimately produces the conclusion that the *rumours of wars* have to complete before Matthew 24:7 and the beginning of the end times (birth pangs) can start is the understanding that Matthew 24 verses 6 and 7 describe two separate events within two separate prophetic time frames. To see them any other way one must ignore the literal instructions Jesus provides within both verses. Because the traditions of men have, in fact, ignored Jesus' literal division of events in verse 6 from those mentioned in 7 and instead have blended them together, the ability to identify Israel as the one who would experience those *rumours of wars* was lost. Therefore, as the war *rumours* swirled about between Israel and Iran (including Lebanon and Gaza) the church is not alert to its significance. And the significance is that Matthew 24:6 is playing out with its *rumours of wars,* which appear can be resolved only through warfare.

However, identifying a war involving Israel that resolves significant *rumours of wars* is only part of what is required to definitively identify such a war as the one which finally resolves Matthew 24:6. Elsewhere we find an additional Scripture that appears to provide another sign linked with that war. It is a celestial sign that appears to be associated with the war that resolves the *rumours of wars* for Israel. According to Scripture, this heavenly sign will be given directly by the Lord. And should it unfold according to this perspective it would act as definitive confirmation that Matthew 24:6 is completing. The sign is discussed by the prophet Joel and is simply described as *wonders in the heavens.*

Prophetic Script

Pre-Birth Pangs Prophetic Time Frame:

1st Rumours of wars for Israel must complete to finish Matthew 24:6. The most likely way for this to be accomplished is an actual war between Israel and Iran, Hamas, and Hezbollah.

CHAPTER TWO

Warnings #1 and #2 Matthew & Joel: A Notable War with a Heavenly Sign

Covered In This Chapter: Why an unusual heavenly sign should be associated with a notable war (Israel-Iran?) and why that would be a very ominous sign.

Covered in this Chapter: Why the "birth pangs" term identifies the beginning phase of the day of the Lord and that it is a de facto announcement of the impending birth of Daniel's 70th week.

Covered in this Chapter: Why both the notable war with a heavenly sign and separately the sun darkening and the moon to blood warn of the impending launch of the day of the Lord (end times).

If war for Israel is necessary to finish Matthew 24:6 by completing notable *rumours of wars,* that perspective may have a confirming sign associated with it distinguishing it from any other war in the history of Israel. This is because the war necessary to complete the *rumours of wars* in Matthew 24:6 appears to be connected to another war which is described in Joel 2:30 and has some kind of unique heavenly sign described in Scripture as *wonders in the heavens.* Consider the case for this by the prophet Joel ...

> *And I will shew wonders in the heavens and in the earth, blood, and fire, and pillars of smoke. Joel 2:30*

This verse tells of a war taking place in the earth with the words ... *and in the earth, blood, and fire, and pillars of smoke* but includes the oddity of some kind of *wonders in the heavens* as well. Why does it appear that this war mentioned in Joel 2:30 is the same war that completed the *rumours of wars* of Matthew 24:6? It is because a literal reading of Matthew 24:7-8, and 1 Thessalonians 5:1-3 appears to connect the war required to complete Matthew 24:6 to the war mentioned in Joel 2:30.

However, in order to see that connection, it is first necessary to appreciate the significance of the term "birth pangs" when used in association with end times prophecy. Without a correct understanding of that term, the ability to follow the beginning phase of end times events does not exist. In addition to appreciating how both Jesus and Paul use the term birth pangs, it is also necessary to understand a basic concept pertaining to *the day of the Lord.* Both will be discussed over the next several pages. Thereafter the connection of *wonders in the heavens* with the war that completes the *rumours of wars* in Matthew 24:6 can be made.

Birth Pangs: The Beginning Phase

Because in Matthew 24 Jesus isolates verse 7 as *the beginning of sorrows,* and then specifically attaches the term birth pangs to describe that *beginning*, it is He who is literally indicating the *beginning* moment, or *beginning* phase of the end times as described in Bible prophecy by the term birth pangs. He is using the term to describe a prophetic time frame and not, as is traditionally taught, a trend of events. This observation that the term describes a prophetic time frame is also supported by the context of Jesus' words wherein suddenness is indicated with the nations needing to *rise* to war. Along with that sudden war is the sudden appearance of famines, pestilences, and earthquakes. Instead of a trend of events, He is relaying a dramatic beginning described in some detail.

Remember that in Matthew 24:4-8 Jesus is responding to specific questions from His apostles. One question is when the end of the current age will take place. In other words, they want to know what will be the signs of the end times beginning. The only way to truly answer that question is to pinpoint the actual moment it all starts. To accomplish pinpointing the moment the end times begin, the first step Jesus takes is to describe what happens just before the actual launch takes place in Matthew verses 4-6. Only after covering what will happen just before it starts does He then describe the events that mark its launch in verse 7. This approach allowed Him to pinpoint *the beginning* and completely fulfill their request.

Therefore, by believing Jesus was specifically answering their question, we have little option other than to accept that the events described in verse 7 are, in fact, the *beginning* moment of what is popularly referred to as the end times. This is highly significant because since He associates the term birth pangs to the actual *beginning* moment of the end times, the term takes on a vastly more significant meaning and usefulness. This is true because once it is concluded that the term birth pangs is used to identify *the beginning* of the end times, then wherever in end times Scripture the term is used it must also be referring to that same prophetic time frame ... the *beginning*. In other words, a birth pangs term identifies a prophetic time frame and is not used to infer trending events.

However, the traditional teaching relating to the term birth pangs must be further addressed here. Those teachings claim that when a birth pangs term appears in Scripture relative to end time prophecy, it is simply indicating a form of "increasing intensity" of events. This teaching is widespread and is the direct result of blending together the pre-birth pangs events in verses 4-6 with the actual birth pangs mentioned in verses 7 and 8. By blending them together it creates a sense that events are trending. This is caused by ignoring Jesus' specific instructions which demarcate the events in verses 4-6 from those in verses 7 and 8. Although this tradition is widespread, it is not supported by Jesus' specific instructions that separate verses 6 and 7 into two completely different events within two completely separate prophetic time frames. This is especially clear not only by the way in which Jesus uses the term birth pangs but by the way Paul does as well.

One rational for claiming a birth pangs term refers to the "increasing intensity" of events is because actual human birth pangs come in waves of increasing severity. Although this is one way of viewing the term birth pangs, it is equally true to say that the moment of human birth pangs also signifies *the beginning* or the arrival of something ... a child. However, in order to determine which one applies to Scripture we should look at the context of how both Jesus and Paul use the term. In the case of Jesus, it is clearly used to indicate *the beginning* because He specifically says this is what it means. Additionally, the events He describes in Matthew 24:7 have a suddenness associated with them and not a trend. And as we see next, Paul uses it in similar fashion. Consider Paul's use of the birth pangs term in 1 Thessalonians 5:1-3.

Paul Confirms Jesus' Use of the Term Birth Pangs

For you yourselves know perfectly that the day of the Lord so cometh as a thief in the night. ³ For when they shall say, Peace and safety; then sudden destruction cometh upon them, <u>as travail upon a woman with child</u>; and they shall not escape.

Because the phrase *as travail upon a woman with child* was used to describe this event, we can understand that it too relates to prophetic birth pangs. And just like Jesus in Matthew 24:8 the Greek word "odin" is used here to signify those birth pangs. So both Jesus in Matthew 24:7-8 and Paul in 1 Thessalonians 5:1-3 describe their events as prophetic birth pangs. And notice how when Paul uses the term birth pangs he associates it with *sudden destruction*. And, of course, such suddenness is the opposite of trending events.

Since we see both Jesus and Paul using the same birth pangs term to describe their respective events, it begs the following question: Would Jesus use a birth pangs term to describe the *beginning of sorrows* and then the Holy Spirit guide Paul to use the birth pangs term to describe events in some time frame other than the *beginning*? Adding to the case that the Holy Spirit is consistent in the use of this term is the fact that when it is used in Matthew we are told the nations will *rise* to go to war. As mentioned earlier, this means they could not already be in a general state of war previous to that moment because they must *rise* to war when the verse begins. That is consistent with what we are being told in 1 Thessalonians 5 where destruction comes suddenly with the words *then sudden destruction cometh upon them,* which logically infers the nations receiving this *sudden destruction* were not already in a state of warfare prior to its beginning. Jesus and Paul both appear to be talking about the same event wherein the nations must *rise* to war in Matthew 24:7, which is the *sudden destruction* described in 1 Thessalonians 5:1-3. War is destruction and the need to *rise* represents a sudden move. *Webster's Dictionary* defines *rise* in this context as "to take up arms." So neither Jesus in Matthew 24:7 or does Paul in 1 Thessalonians 5:1-3 infer anything other than suddenness when using the term birth pangs and they both appear to be describing the same *beginning* event.

Adding to the case that the Holy Spirit is consistent in using the birth pangs term to denote the *beginning* of the end times is that we are told the *sudden destruction* in 1 Thessalonians 5 *cometh as a thief in the night,* which amplifies its suddenness. But consider this- If this is not the opening event of the end times, how then could it come with such surprise? Remember, during the end times along with great physical destruction of property a large portion of the world's population is lost. Within such an environment how could this verse unfold with the suddenness of *a thief in the night* if it occurs deep into the end times after so many horrific events have already occurred? It could not. It is only during the *beginning of sorrows* that such surprise is possible. In strategic terms this is called the "element of surprise." Once great cataclysms begin unfolding, the element of surprise is lost.

So both Jesus and Paul painstakingly set out to describe their respective events as the *beginning* of the end times and then label them as birth pangs. However, there is one more concept that must briefly be dealt with before connecting Joel's *wonders in the heavens* to the war that completes Matthew 24:6.

CRITICAL CONCLUSION: THE TERM BIRTH PANGS IDENTIFIES A SPECIFIC END TIMES PROPHETIC TIME FRAME ... THE BEGINNING.

Some teach that the events in 1 Thessalonians 5:1-3 must happen much later in the end times because they are described as *the day of the Lord.* This is taught in spite of those events being associated here with birth pangs, as well as its beginning coming suddenly and *as a thief in the night,* all of which speak to it occurring at the beginning moment of the end times. Part of the reason for this misconception is because within Zachariah 14 we find *the day of the Lord* associated with the moment Jesus sets foot on the Mount of Olives, which is an event that clearly happens deep into the end times. The resolution to this apparent contradiction is quite simple. The term *the day of the Lord* also represents a time frame and not one specific event. It is the entirety of what is popularly referred to as the end times from its starting point until its ending point. People just use the term end times to denote it. But more accurately they should say *the day of the Lord* instead of the end times.

The reason we know *the day of the Lord* covers the entirety of all end times events from start to finish is because we see in 1 Thessalonians 5 an event that is the literal launch of the end times even coming *as a thief in the night* described as *the day of the Lord,* and then we also find Zechariah 14, which tells us that *the day of the Lord* also encompasses the moment Jesus sets foot on the Mount of Olives, which is close to the final moment of the end times. Along with Zechariah 14, it appears that Isaiah 34 and Zechariah 12 also describe that same event much later in *the day of the Lord,* and none of those chapters possess a birth pangs term within them. So we see *the day of the Lord* covering the entire time frame of what is popularly referred to as the end times stretching from its literal start until its finish.

Therefore, in order to differentiate the starting point or beginning phase of events in *the day of the Lord* a birth pangs term is used. It is that simple. So when we say the end times we are really saying *the day of the Lord* and when the birth pangs term is applied to it we are talking about the beginning phase of *the day of the Lord.* That is why within Zechariah chapters 12 and 14 as well as Isaiah 34 there are no birth pangs terms found anywhere within those entire chapters because they relay events that take place near the end of *the day of the Lord.* Whereas we see that within 1 Thessalonians 5:1-3 and an array of additional Scriptures soon to be looked at we see events at the beginning of *the day of the Lord* and find the birth pangs term within them. We begin looking at those Scriptures next. So *the day of the Lord* is the broad time frame encompassing the entirety of what is popularly referred to as the end times and the term birth pangs is used to segment the beginning phase of it from the remainder. Further confirmation that *the day of the Lord* (end times) has a beginning phase distinguished by the term birth pangs is the structure of the Book of Revelation.

The entire catalogue of horrific events within the Book of Revelation is produced from seven seals opened in heaven by the hand of Jesus. However, those horrific events do not begin until chapter 6, wherein six of the seven seals are opened in that single chapter, unleashing the Four Horsemen of the Apocalypse among other things. It is a clear beginning of the end times that we see in Revelation 6. And the events in Revelation 6 have a striking resemblance to Jesus' description of events in Matthew 24:7, which He describes as *the beginning* and birth pangs. However, whereas six of those seven seals are opened in that one chapter, the seventh seal remains unopened until chapter 8. Those events in chapter 6, which are so similar to the events described by Jesus in Matthew 24:7, are segregated in the Book of Revelation from the seventh seal. And it is from that seventh seal that all remaining horrific judgments in Revelation are unleashed, including the seven trumpets and seven bowl judgments. In other words, 6 judgments are unleashed in chapter 6 and then beginning in chapter 8 the remaining 14 judgments are unleashed. This structure of segregating events in the Book of Revelation that are strikingly similar to Matthew's birth pang events from all other end times events in Revelation supports their separate nature. Consider a final Scripture that clearly uses the birth pangs term to denote the beginning.

In Isaiah 42:13-15, the Lord declares His intent to prevail against his enemies in a time past. Although this is not referring to *the day of the Lord*, it is the usage of a birth pangs term here that gets our attention:

---

13 The Lord shall go forth as a mighty man, he shall stir up jealousy like a man of war: he shall cry, yea, roar; he shall prevail against his enemies.

---

14 I have long time holden my peace; I have been still, and refrained myself: now will I cry like a travailing woman; I will destroy and devour at once.

---

15 I will make waste mountains and hills, and dry up all their herbs; and I will make the rivers islands, and I will dry up the pools.

In verse 14 after bemoaning how He has held His *peace, been still, and reframed myself*, but He is now ready to begin dealing with His enemies. After telling us of this intent, He associates the beginning of His actions with the birth pangs term *like a travailing woman*. So here too we see the birth pangs term used to identify the beginning of His wrath against an enemy.

> CRITICAL CONCLUSION: *THE DAY OF THE LORD* INCLUDES THE ENTIRETY OF WHAT IS REFERRED TO AS THE END TIMES FROM ITS STARTING MOMENT UNTIL ITS FINAL MOMENT.

> CRITICAL CONCLUSION: THE TERM BIRTH PANGS IDENTIFIES THE BEFINNING PHASE OF *THE DAY OF THE LORD*.

Why an Israel-Iran War (resolving rumours of wars) May Include a Heavenly Sign

We covered in chapter one why an Israel-Iran war may be a Scriptural necessity. Now we will look at why in Scripture that particular war appears to have some kind of heavenly sign associated with it. This connection begins with the understanding that the birth pangs term, when used within the context of *the day of the Lord*, represents its beginning phase and is demarcated from the rest of end time events. With this understanding we see that a literal read of Scripture indicates the war that resolves the *rumours of wars* of Matthew 24:6 may include some kind of sign in the heavens as well. For that conclusion we now turn our attention to the Book of Joel.

It is in Joel 2:30-31 wherein those two verses describe a notable war in verse 30 followed by a sign coming just before *the day of the Lord* in verse 31. Since it relates to events just before the beginning of *the day of the Lord*, it must be connected to 1 Thessalonians 5:1-3, which also looks at the beginning of *the day of the Lord* by including the birth pangs term. Joel 2:30-31 must also be connected to Matthew 24:7-8 since it is connected to the same beginning of *the day of the Lord* by possessing the birth pangs term within it as well. But Joel does not need to use the birth pangs term in these verses because he states that what he is writing about comes just before *the day of the Lord*, indicating that its beginning is very close. Consider Joel 2:30 first.

> *And I will shew wonders in the heavens and in the earth, blood, and fire, and pillars of smoke. Joel 2:30*

This verse is literally telling us of a war on the earth with the words *in the earth, blood, and fire, and pillars of smoke* before the start of *the day of the Lord.* This war must be notable since it is being identified by Scripture. In addition to this notable war on the earth, there will be some kind of heavenly sign associated with it or, as the Scripture tells us, *wonders in the heavens* either before or during that war. Then the next major event to unfold before the start of *the day of the Lord* is ...

The sun shall be turned into darkness, and the moon into blood, <u>before</u> the great and terrible <u>day of the LORD come.</u> Joel 2:31

We are being told that also *before* the beginning of *the day of the Lord* a certain celestial sign will take place. This sign involves the sun and the moon telling us: *The sun shall be turned into darkness, and the moon into blood.* Remember, we have connected the beginning of *the day of the Lord* with the great war of Matthew 24:7 as well as the *sudden destruction* of 1 Thessalonians 5:2-3. This is because Jesus, in Matthew 24:7-8, describes the great war wherein *nation shall rise against nation* as birth pangs, just as 1 Thessalonians 5:2-3 attaches the same birth pangs term with the *sudden destruction* that starts *the day of the Lord.* Therefore, Joel 2:31 is referencing the approach of the beginning of *the day of the Lord* and Matthew 24:7 is speaking to the start of *the day of the Lord.* Now pay close attention to this.

> CRITICAL CONCLUSION: THE SCRIPTURES JOEL 2:31, MAT-
> THEW 24:7, AND 1 THESSALONIANS 5:1-3 ALL DESCRIBE EVENTS
> OCCURRING JUST BEFORE *THE DAY OF THE LORD* LAUNCHES
> AND/OR ITS BEGINNING EVENTS

A Notable War Followed By a Great War

We see that both Matthew 24:6-8 and Joel 2:30-31 describe the exact same sequence of events wherein there is a notable war followed by the launch of *the day of the Lord.* We have reasoned that the most likely way for Israel to bring to an end the *rumours of wars* to complete Matthew 24:6 is an actual war with the nation she had been embroiled within those *rumours* with ... Iran. Then in Matthew 24:7 we see the next event that unfolds is a great war where *nation shall rise against nation, and kingdom against kingdom* and since it is described as birth pangs can only be the start of *the day of the Lord.* This connection to the beginning of *the day of the Lord* was made as a result of Matthew's connection to 1 Thessalonians 5:1-3, where the same birth pangs term is used to describe the start of *the day of the Lord.* So what we have in Matthew 24:6-8 is the following:

Matthew 24:6-8

1st Notable war

2nd *The day of the Lord* launches

Now consider what Joel 2:30-31 is telling us.

In Joel 2:30 we are told of a notable war with the words *in the earth, blood, and fire, and pillars of smoke* and then next we are told about the approach of *the day of the Lord,* which we know launches with a great war. So within both Scriptural readings, Matthew 24:6-8 and also Joel 2:30-31, we see a description of the same sequence of events: a notable war followed by the war that begins *the day of the Lord.* Since Jesus' words logically infer, and His prophet Joel's words describe a notable war just prior to the launch of the great war that starts *the day of the Lord,* then we must believe the Holy Spirit is being consistent and orderly here and that both are talking about the same notable war but simply from different perspectives. So what we have in Matthew 24:6-8 and Joel 2:30-31 is this:

Matthew 24:6-8	**Joel 2:30-31**
1st Notable war	1st Notable war
2nd *The day of the Lord* launches	2nd *The day of the Lord* launches

Within both Matthew 24:6-8 and Joel 30-31 are relayed the exact same sequence of events. Both indicate there will be a notable war which comes before the great war that starts *the day of the Lord.* These two Scriptures are used to provide different perspectives and information on that notable war. And it is the unique descriptions provided by both Matthew and Joel which allow that war to be identified as the one that comes just before the launch of *the day of the Lord.*

Matthew and Joel's Perspectives

From the perspective of Matthew 24:6 presented here it appears that this notable war will involve Israel and is preceded by significant *rumours of wars* which must be resolved, and this has allowed us to identify the nation of Iran as the most likely nation to be involved in that war with Israel to resolve the verse. And we also know that since Matthew 24:6 is in a prophetic time frame just prior to the launch of *the day of the Lord,* it must be resolved first. However, Joel tells us that the same war which comes just before *the day of the Lord* will have associated with it some kind of *wonders in the heavens.* And since this war in Joel 2:30 happens just before the launch of *the day of the Lord* it too is in the pre-birth pangs prophetic time frame. So Matthew 24:6 and Joel 2:30 should be the same war being described but from different perspectives.

If this reasoning is correct, then it appears that the Lord purposely connected such an unmistakable sign so that mankind would not confuse the war that resolved Matthew 24:6 with any previous Israeli war. Essentially, that combination of events (an Israeli war resolving notable *rumours of wars* combined with *wonders in the heavens*) is so improbable it causes that war to be segregated from all other Israeli wars as the notable one being waited for.

> CRITICAL CONCLUSION: THE WAR REQUIRED TO RESOLVE MATTHEW 24:6 IS THE SAME WAR DESCRIBED IN JOEL 2:30 AND WILL HAVE A HEAVENLY SIGN ASSOCIATED WITH IT.

Prophetic Script

Pre-Birth Pangs Prophetic Time Frame:

1st Rumours of wars for Israel must complete to finish Matthew 24:6. The most likely way for this to be accomplished is an actual war between Israel and Iran, Hamas, and Hezbollah.

Warning I ... Before the "End Times" Launch

2nd (Added this chapter) A notable war (possibly Israel-Iran) that has associated with it some kind of wonders in the heavens. Exactly what these wonders are is not given.

Warning II ... Before the "End Times" Launch

3rd (Added this chapter) The sun shall turn into darkness and the moon into blood (possibly a time of notable solar eclipses and blood moons) before the great war that launches the day of the Lord.

Warning #3

U.N. "Peace" Agreement: The Final Warning before the End Times Launch

CHAPTER THREE

Warning #3
Joel: "All Nations" (U.N.)
Peace Agreement ... The
Final Warning

Covered in this Chapter: Why it is a peace agreement initiated by all nations removing land from Israel, which is the final warning before the great war that begins the day of the Lord (end times).

Covered in this Chapter: Why the Antichrist does not initiate but confirms an agreement that was previously made by all nations.

Covered in this Chapter: Why before the day of the Lord begins there will be two celestial signs.

Covered in this Chapter: Why during the day of the Lord there will be a celestial condition distinct from the celestial sign before it begins.

By establishing the significance of the birth pangs term we find evidence for the next and final geopolitical event that takes place just before the start of *the day of the Lord.* That last sign is a grand *Peace* agreement initiated by *all nations,* which results in the removal of a portion of land from Israel.

The conclusion that it is *all nations* who originate, initiate, or make this agreement runs counter to another belief embraced within certain prophecy circles. The tradition holds that it is the Antichrist who initiates, makes, or creates the *Peace* agreement. However, when the Scriptures are read literally and within context, it is clear that it is *all nations* that initiate the agreement and the Antichrist is the one who will *confirm* it sometime later. This is why, in referring to the initial agreement, the prophet Daniel (Daniel 9:27) literally tells us the Antichrist will *confirm* it and not initiate it. Then he alludes to the original agreement initiated by *all nations* by describing the one Antichrist will *confirm* as *the covenant with many*. By alerting us that *many* nations will be involved in the initial agreement, Daniel is establishing the context of how we should read an array of other Scriptures which relate to this agreement. With that context in mind, we will see that it can only be *all nations* that initiate this agreement.

All Nations (U.N.) Initiates the Peace Agreement

Because 1 Thessalonians 5:2-3 tells us: *For when they shall say, Peace and safety; then sudden destruction cometh upon them,* we see a key signpost appearing just before the start of *the day of the Lord*. It is a *Peace* agreement. We know this happens before it launches because only after *they say Peace* (covenant) then does *the day of the Lord* start, wherein *sudden destruction cometh upon them.* So it would appear that after Israel concludes Matthew 24:6 and the *rumours of wars,* thereafter she will be involved in a notable *Peace* agreement before the launch of *the day of the Lord*. That *Peace* agreement is the final signpost that the horrific *day of the Lord* is about to begin with *sudden destruction* in which Jesus in Matthew 24:7 tells us *nation shall rise against nation* as it starts.

Although 1 Thessalonians 5:1-3 mentions the *Peace* agreement coming just before the launch of *the day of the Lord,* it also alludes to who will initiate this agreement against Israel. Consider verse 3 and keep in mind the description by Daniel (9:27) that the initial agreement involves *many* by referring to it as *the covenant with many*.

> [3] *For when they shall say, Peace and safety; then sudden destruction cometh upon them, as travail upon a woman with child; and they shall not escape. 1 Thessalonians 5:3*

Notice that all references of who is involved in this agreement are plural and not singular. The Scripture doesn't allude to it being a single individual such as the Antichrist by reading "For when **he** shall say" but infers many will be involved in it by reading *For when **they** shall say.* Because of the wording in this verse it is very easy to impart a multitude being involved in the initiation of this agreement by the fact it is **they** who say its peace resulting in destruction upon **them** and **they** will not escape.

With 1 Thessalonians 5:3 inferring a number of nations involved in the agreement, and Daniel referring to the agreement as the *covenant with **many***, we will now look at other Scriptures connected by the common link of the birth pangs term to confirm that a multitude of nations initiate this agreement. The prophets that directly tell us this are Joel and Jeremiah. The prophet Joel describes what happens just before *the day of the Lord* launches. Then two verses later he tells us the reason for the launch of *the day of the Lord* (end times) and as will be seen, it is because *all nations... parted my land* with no sign of warfare.

In the case of Jeremiah he uses the birth pangs term within chapter 30, thereby placing the events he is describing as within the beginning phase of *the day of the Lord* (end times). Then we have an additional prophet who indirectly and contextually alludes to it being *all nations* that initiate this agreement. He is the prophet Isaiah. So the conclusion that it is *all nations* that initiate the *Peace* agreement is strongly supported by a multitude of Scriptures when read literally and within context. And with the appearance of the United Nations in the year 1947, *all nations* can now fulfill this prophecy perfectly for the first time in world history. And keep in mind that Daniel 9:27 establishes the proper context of whom it is that initiates the agreement when he describes it as a *covenant with many*. Now we look at those other Scriptures to specifically find who initiates the *covenant with many*, which the Antichrist will eventually *confirm*.

After the Jews Return to the Land

In the last chapter we connected the *wonders in the heavens* and the *sun* and *moon* signs in Joel 2:30-31 to the events described by Jesus in Matthew 24:6-8. Both describe the same sequence of events including a notable war followed by the launch of *the day of the Lord*. However, Joel goes on to tell us the time frame wherein those two events will happen. Thereafter in the next verse he tells us the reason for the launch of *the day of the Lord*. First, consider the time frame he provides.

For, behold, in those days, and in that time, when I shall bring again the captivity of Judah and Jerusalem. Joel 3:1

Immediately after describing the notable war followed by the beginning of *the day of the Lord* two verses earlier in Joel 2:31, here in Joel 3:1 the prophet references back to those events by beginning this verse 3:1 with the words: *For, behold, in those days, and in that time ...* So it appears Joel 3:1 is establishing that both the notable war, later followed by the launch of *the day of the Lord* described in Joel 2:30-31, will take place after the Jews are returned to Judah and Jerusalem. This gives us the reference dates of 1948, when they returned as a nation, and 1967, when the eastern half of Jerusalem was restored to Israeli control, giving them control over the entire city for the first time in almost 2,000 years. How do we know Joel 3:1 is referring to the Jews returning to the land instead of being taken captive again as the wording in the verse implies? It is because Jeremiah 30:3 resolves that question by using virtually the same wording saying, ... *I will bring again the captivity of my people Israel and Judah, saith the Lord: and will cause them to return to the land that I gave their fathers* ... So all of the events described in Joel 2:30-31, a *war on the earth* and thereafter *the day of the Lord,* occur after the Jews are returned to the land and regain control over Judah and the city of Jerusalem. Since we know Judah and Jerusalem came back under Israeli control in 1967 during the Six-Day War, we are being told *the day of the Lord* will happen sometime after that year.

> CRITICAL CONCLUSION: FROM A PROPHETIC STANDPOINT,
> THE CRITICAL MOMENT IS WHEN THE JEWS RETURN TO JUDAH
> AND JERUSALEM.

Now the prophet is ready to provide the specifics of <u>why</u> after the Jews return to the land *the day of the Lord* takes place. And it is the answer to that question that gives us another detail of the *Peace* agreement mentioned in 1 Thessalonians 5:1-3, which happens just before the great war that launches *the day of the Lord.* It also begins to identify Daniel's *covenant with many* that the Antichrist will eventually *confirm.*

All nations ... parted my land

When reading the next verse, notice there is no mention of warfare against Israel within it. Also continue to keep in mind as you read this verse in Joel that Daniel 9:27 described the agreement the Antichrist would eventually *confirm* as *the covenant with many.* So we are looking for that initial *covenant with many* that the Antichrist will later *confirm.* That observation is the key to placing the events being described in Joel 3:2 within the proper context. So let's continue now.

After just having told us in the previous verse the general time frame of when *the day of the Lord* (end times) will take place, the next verse proceeds with the words: *I will also* ... indicating a continuation of the previous thought.

<u>*I will also*</u> *gather* <u>*all nations,*</u> *and will bring them down into the valley of Jehoshaphat, and will plead with them there for my people and for my heritage Israel, whom they have scattered among the nations, and* <u>*parted my land.*</u> *Joel 3:2*

In this verse we are told the *valley of Jehoshaphat* is being used as the theatre of God's judgment against *all nations.* We are being told who is being punished at the beginning of *the day of the Lord* (end times) and it is *all nations.* In agreement with this punishment directed toward the nations, remember that in Matthew 24:7 we found that *nation shall rise against nation* ... at the beginning of *the day of the Lord.*

So we immediately see agreement between Joel and Matthew as both speak about the beginning of *the day of the Lord* and who it is being dealt with. Now consider what is meant by the *valley of Jehoshaphat*. *Strong's Concordance* defines *Jehoshaphat* used in this context as "Jehovah has judged." It is highly unlikely that this is a literal valley located somewhere near Israel. In fact, *Strong's* adds the comment that its usage here is a "symbolical name of a valley near Jerusalem." So the nations are not gathered into a literal valley for punishment but into the valley of the Lord's judgment. Notice, this is not *all nations* coming into a *valley* called *Jehoshaphat* to take land from Israel. It was already *parted* as opposed to conquered. Instead we are told that Jehovah is judging them in the *valley of Jehoshaphat* for having *parted my land.*

We are literally being told here why *the day of the Lord* (end times) launched, and it is because *all nations ... parted* the land of Israel without any indication it was conquered by an army. Since there is no mention of warfare against Israel and the term *parted* is used instead of *conquered,* it could only be *parted* by a settlement or an agreement of some kind. The word used for *parted* in the verse is the Hebrew verb "chalac" which means "to divide, apportion, assign, distribute, impart or share" all of which indicate non-conflict was used to divide the land. This conclusion is the result of a literal read of the verse without adding anything to it.

There are only two ways a nation can lose land. The first is through warfare where the vanquished lose tracts of land to an invading army. The only other way for a nation to lose land is for the land to be removed by an agreement. By reading this verse with a literal eye, we see nowhere the mention of armed conflict as being the reason for the land being *parted.* Believing that the Lord spoke it with Divine precision to His prophet, we must accept that it could only be *parted* or divided by an agreement. And currently on the event horizon, there is an omen of this coming because the goal of the United Nations (*all nations*) is to remove some of the land from Israel in the name of *Peace.* And it is the United Nations that represents *all nations* just as the prophet tells us to look for.

Note that since the parting of the land already took place, it happens <u>before</u> *the day of the Lord* begins and is accomplished without warfare. This confirms what we read in 1 Thessalonians 5:1-3 where *sudden destruction* launching *the day of the Lord* comes only <u>after</u> *they say Peace.* And all efforts at *Peace* in the Middle East conflict since the year 1990 revolve around the notion that it will result only by removing land from Israel. The Scriptures are telling us it is the removal of land from Israel by *all nations* that is the reason for the start of great war that begins *the day of the Lord* (end times). That *Peace* agreement by *all nations* represents the final warning.

CRITICAL CONCLUSION: JOEL IS TELLING US THAT *ALL NA-TIONS* WILL DIVIDE THE LAND OF ISRAEL WITHOUT WARFARE. THIS ACTION LAUNCHES THE BIRTH PANGS OR BEGINNING PHASE OF *THE DAY OF THE LORD* (END TIMES)

Scriptural Harmony: Matthew 24:6-8 and 1 Thessalonians 5:1-3 and Joel 2:30-3:2

Follow this carefully with one eye on what we have already covered and keep in mind it is all based on a very literal reading of the Scriptures. We have read in 1 Thessalonians 5:1-3 that *they* will make a *Peace* agreement just before the *sudden destruction* that launches *the day of the Lord,* and Joel is telling us the reason for the launch of *the day of the Lord* is that *all nations parted* the land. Since Joel does not mention warfare being used to part the land then only an agreement of some kind could accomplish it which is perfectly in line with what 1 Thessalonians 5 says. Remember, it is *all nations* being gathered in the symbolical *valley of Jehoshaphat* for punishment in Joel 3:2 but only AFTER they have *parted* the land. Therefore, both Joel and also 1 Thessalonians 5 are indicating that just before *the day of the Lord* begins there will be an agreement removing some land from Israel. However, Joel adds the critical detail that it will be *all nations* who initiate that *Peace* agreement which is in harmony with 1 Thessalonians 5:3 which says *they* will initiate the agreement. Additionally we also see Joel connected to Matthew 24:7. In Matthew we see *nation shall rise against nation, and kingdom against kingdom,* indicating a great multitude of nations going to war, which also sounds a lot like *all nations.* We have already connected Matthew 24:7 to the start of *the day of the Lord* because Jesus describes those sudden events as birth pangs. Joel is also describing the beginning of *the day of the Lord.* We see harmony between Matthew's multitude of nations going to war against one another and *all nations* being punished in Joel, and 1 Thessalonians 5:3 referring in the plural to those who make the agreement as *they.* So Matthew 24:6-8, 1 Thessalonians 5:1-3, and Joel 2:30-31 and 3:1-2 are all witnessing it will be a multitude of nations that will initiate the agreement. And, of course, all of this is in line with Daniel 9:27 which the agreement that the Antichrist will *confirm* (not initiate) is described as *the covenant with many.*

CRITICAL CONCLUSION: THERE IS HARMONY BETWEEN MATTHEW 24:7, JOEL 3:2, AND 1 THESSALONIANS 5:1-3.

Three Celestial signs associated with the Day of the Lord

It is indicated in Joel 2:30-31 that two celestial signs will occur <u>before</u> the launch of *the day of the Lord*. Those warnings consist of *wonders in the heavens* in association with a notable war on the earth, and the second celestial sign is the *sun shall be turned into darkness, and the moon into blood*. Exactly what these signs will consist of is not made clear. Although both celestial events of Joel 2:30-31 take place *<u>before</u> the day of the Lord*, it is important to understand that there is a celestial <u>condition</u> that develops during *the day of the Lord* that is probably a result of the horrific events that take place within it. Unless this is understood, much confusion results when studying celestial signs relative to *the day of the Lord*. This celestial condition during *the day of the Lord* appears to be caused by the atmosphere being impacted by the events that accompany it. But first consider again Joel 2:30-31 and the two celestial warnings coming *<u>before</u> the day of the Lord*.

> *³⁰ And I will shew wonders in the heavens and in the earth, blood, and fire, and pillars of smoke.*

> *The sun shall be turned into darkness, and the moon into blood, <u>before</u> the great and terrible day of the LORD come.*
> *Joel 2:31*

And now consider Acts 2:20, the second Scripture to confirm this.

> *¹⁹ And I will shew wonders in heaven above, and signs in the earth beneath; blood, and fire, and vapour of smoke:*

> *²⁰ The sun shall be turned into darkness, and the moon into blood, before the great and notable day of the Lord come:*
> *Acts 2:20*

So we know that <u>before</u> *the day of the Lord* launches there will take place some kind of *wonders in the heavens* associated with a notable war on the earth as well as the *sun* darkening and the *moon into blood.* However, the celestial condition which unfolds <u>during</u> *the day of the Lord* includes not only the *sun* and the *moon* but also the *stars*. And this is an important distinction since whereas the sun and moon are impacted by eclipses, the stars are not. The apparent reason why all three-the *sun, moon,* and *stars* are impacted <u>during</u> *the day of the Lord* is explained in Joel 2:1-2 and Zephaniah 1:15 and has to do with the condition of the atmosphere during that time.

---

[1]... for the day of the Lord cometh, for it is nigh at hand;

---

[2]A day of darkness and of gloominess, a day of clouds and of thick darkness, as the morning spread upon the mountains: ... Joel 2:1-2

Zephaniah 1:15 uses virtually the same wording to confirm this saying:

---

[15] That day is a day of wrath, a day of trouble and distress, a day of wasteness and desolation, a day of darkness and gloominess, a day of clouds and thick darkness,

---

This atmospheric impact being described in both verses happens <u>during</u> *the day of the Lord* and is completely unrelated to the celestial signs coming <u>before</u> it starts. Consider the following Scriptures relating to the impact this *day of clouds and thick darkness* has in the celestial signs <u>during</u> *the day of the Lord.*

Celestial Sign: During the Day of the Lord

Since we are told that *the day of the Lord* is *a day of clouds and thick darkness,* we can logically deduct that its impact will extend beyond the *sun and moon* and include the *stars* as well. In line with that reasoning, consider the following Scriptures as they relate to *the day of the Lord.*

---

[10] The earth shall quake before them; the heavens shall tremble: the sun and the moon shall be dark, and the stars shall withdraw their shining: Joel 2:10

Due to the atmospheric conditions detailed in Joel 2:1-2 and Zephaniah 1:15, we see that <u>during</u> *the day of the Lord* (end times) the *sun, moon,* and *stars* are all impacted from this *day of clouds and thick darkness.* We are also told *The earth shall quake,* which is in agreement with our perspective that Matthew 24:7 marks the launch of *the day of the Lord* because it too describes *earthquakes*. There is harmony between Joel 2:10 and Matthew 24:7.

Now consider Matthew 24:29.

> ²⁹ *Immediately after the tribulation of those days shall the sun be darkened, and the moon shall not give her light, and the stars shall fall from heaven, and the powers of the heavens shall be shaken:*

Remember, this verse in Matthew is well into chapter 24 and we know that *the day of the Lord* (end times) began back in verse 7. <u>During</u> *the day of the Lord* there is great tribulation and we can see this Scripture as further confirmation that all three- the *sun, moon,* and *stars* are impacted <u>during</u> that time. The description that *the stars shall fall from heaven* must be referring to them taking a "great fall" as in disappearing and not literally falling onto the earth, which would be an unreasonable conclusion.

So the first two celestial events are wonders in the heavens and then a sign in the *sun* and *moon* just <u>before</u> the launch of *the day of the Lord* (end times). But <u>during</u> *the day of the Lord* the *sun, moon,* and *stars* are impacted. Exactly what the *wonders in the heavens* sign will consist of is not clear. But the other celestial sign <u>before</u> *the day of the Lord* begins might be eclipses involving both the *sun* and *moon,* causing the sun to be *turned into darkness, and the moon into blood.* This explanation seems to make the most sense because nowhere in Scripture is there any reported thick clouds in the atmosphere <u>before</u> *the day of the Lord* begins. Also, in both cases where this particular sign coming <u>before</u> is provided, it only includes the sun and moon and not the stars. However, <u>during</u> *the day of the Lord* it is impossible that the impact on the *sun, moon,* and *stars* comes from eclipses because the stars are impacted as well. And, of course, only the *sun* and *moon* can be impacted by eclipses, which leave the *clouds and thick darkness* as the most logical reason for all three being impacted <u>during</u> *the day of the Lord* (end times). So wherever we are told the *sun, moon,* and *stars* are impacted, it occurs <u>during</u> *the day of the Lord* and is a distinction worth remembering.

Prophetic Script

1st Rumours of wars for Israel must complete to finish Matthew 24:6. The most likely way for this to be accomplished is an actual war between Israel and Iran, Hamas, and Hezbollah.

2nd (Added this chapter) A notable war (possibly Israel-Iran) that has associated with it some kind of wonders in the heavens. Exactly what these wonders are is not given.

3rd (Added this chapter) The sun shall turn into darkness and the moon into blood (possibly a time of notable solar eclipses and blood moons) before the great war that launches the day of the Lord.

4th Next, All nations initiate an agreement removing land from Israel in the name of Peace.

1st (Added this chapter) Next The day of the Lord launches with a great-war sometime after that Peace agreement initiated by all nations.

2nd (Added this chapter) The great war between the nations that launches the day of the Lord comes with a thief in the night kind of surprise and includes great earthquakes, famines, pestilences, and thick darkness across the world making it difficult at times to see the sun, moon, and stars.

CHAPTER FOUR

Jeremiah: Confirms the Final Warning

Covered in this Chapter: Jeremiah confirms it is a peace treaty initiated by *all nations* (U.N.) removing land from Israel that is the final warning just before the great war that launches *the day of the Lord.*

W e are told in 2 Corinthians 13:1 that ... *In the mouth of two or three witnesses shall every word be established.* And it is important to understand that a good witness does not embellish their words but relays them as accurately (literally) as possible. So far we have the prophet Joel indicating it will be *all nations* who the Lord punishes because they *part*ed the land of Israel prior to the launch of *the day of the Lord* (end times). We see that this parting of the land is without warfare against Israel, indicating only an agreement or covenant could accomplish it. And this is the reason given for the launch of *the day of the Lord.* Contextually we also see Matthew 24:7 and also 1 Thessalonians 5:1-3 coming into harmony with this perspective. Matthew shows that a multitude of nations suffer a great war during the terrible birth pangs beginning phase of *the day of the Lord* and 1 Thessalonians alerts us that just before *the day of the Lord* that *they* will proclaim a *Peace* agreement. Now we shall add another witness to this rendition---the prophet Jeremiah. Consider his words carefully in relation to how he confirms what Joel said. Also keep in mind the words of Daniel 9:27, wherein we are told that the Antichrist will *confirm* and not initiate an agreement Daniel refers to as *the covenant with many.* And Daniel's description of the agreement as the *covenant with many* highlights its notable characteristic that a multitude of nations will be involved in it. With that perspective in mind, we have the proper context to read Jeremiah 30.

> *For, lo, the days come, saith the LORD, that I will bring again the captivity of my people Israel and Judah, saith the LORD: and I will cause them to return to the land that I gave to their fathers, and they shall possess it. Jeremiah 30:3*

What time frame is Jeremiah talking about? It is when the Jews are returned *Israel and Judah* which began unfolding in 1948. Consider when reading this verse that Joel 3:1 uses almost the same phrase, indicating that the events being discussed in both Joel and Jeremiah are referring to the same time frame. This establishes the first sign of harmony between the two prophets. Remember in Joel 3:1 after establishing this time frame we were told in the next verse, Joel 3:2, that great punishment for *all nations* takes place because they *parted my land.* And with no sign of warfare anywhere within the verse to accomplish the parting, it could only have been done by an agreement of some kind. Keep in mind that perspective of Joel and also Daniel's description of the initial agreement as *the covenant with many* when you read these Scriptures in Jeremiah 30 for the proper context.

> *Ask ye now, and see whether a man doth travail with child?*
> *Wherefore do I see every man with his hands on his loins, as*
> *a <u>woman in travail</u>, and all faces are turned into paleness?*
> *⁷Alas! For that day is great, so none is like it: it is even <u>the</u>*
> *<u>time of Jacob's trouble</u>, but he shall be saved out of it. Jere-*
> *miah 30:6-7*

The events being described in this Scripture are *the time of Jacob's trouble,* another way of saying *the day of the Lord* (end times). We know these Scriptures are identifying the beginning phase of *the day of the Lord* because the words *woman in travail* is a birth pangs phrase. The word used to denote it is "yalad," Hebrew for "of child birth," "to be born," "to beget a child." Since a birth pangs term was used here, we should see Jeremiah 30 come into harmony with what Matthew 24:7-8, 1 Thessalonians 5:1-3, and Joel 3:1-2 have been saying relative to a great war launching *the day of the Lord* after *all nations* remove land from Israel in a *Peace* agreement of some kind.

> *For I am with thee, saith the Lord, to save thee: though I*
> *make a full end of <u>all nations</u> whither I have scattered thee,*
> *yet I will not make a full end of thee: but I will <u>correct thee</u>*
> *<u>in measure</u>, and will not leave thee altogether unpunished.*
> *Jeremiah 30:11*

Once again we see that *all nations* are being punished by the Lord. This is the same *all nations* mentioned in Joel 3:2 and inferred in Matthew's multitude of nations going to war. In fact, Jeremiah observes a severe punishment as indicated that the Lord will *make a full end of all nations whither I have scattered thee.* The reference *whither I have scattered thee* refers to the multitude of nations across the earth where the Jews had previously been scattered during the Diaspora. So both Jeremiah and Joel mention *all nations* being punished, which is harmonious with Matthew's multitude of nations suffering a great war. And all of these Scriptures indicate these events take place in the beginning of *the day of the Lord* (end times) because they either possess a birth pangs reference or tell us they happen at its beginning.

But strangely we are told by Jeremiah that *thee* is also being punished but *in measure.* Who are *thee?* It is Israel. Why is Israel receiving punishment along with *all nations?* Notice that the punishment *all nations* receive is extremely severe, with the Lord promising to *make a full end of* them. Israel, on the other hand, is only punished *in measure.* The answer to that question comes out in verse 16.

> Therefore, they that devour thee *shall be devoured; and all*
> *thine adversaries, every one of them, shall go into captivity;*
> *and they that* spoil *thee shall be a spoil, and all that* prey
> *upon thee will I give for prey. Jeremiah 30:16*

The reason for the *full end* of *all nations* comes out in verse 16 and it is because they *devour* Israel. The only way to *devour* Israel is to remove some of her land. We know all of the land was not removed because God is punishing Israel after *all nations devour* her. Just as in Joel 3:2, here too there is no indication in this verse or this entire chapter of Jeremiah that warfare is used against Israel to *devour* her land. In other words, this removal of the land did not happen through force-of-arms. Israel was not conquered. Without war the removal of land from a nation can only happen through an agreement of some kind. The only kind of agreement that would result in Israel giving up land is an agreement in the name of *Peace,* which is exactly what the United Nations *(all nations)* has been seeking to do. The word used here for *devour* is the Hebrew verb "akal" meaning "to devour or eat." This verb is used throughout the Scriptures but never in association with military conquest. The word for *spoil* is the Hebrew verb "sha'ac," which means to "plunder" or be "robbed." The word for *prey* is the Hebrew verb "bazaz," which means to "prey upon or seize." So the context of the explanation as to why *all nations* are being punished at the beginning of *the day of the Lord* in this chapter is related to "seizing" the land but not conquering it.

Understanding that only a *Peace* agreement can *devour* the land of Israel in Jeremiah 30, explains why Israel is also being punished. For such a *Peace* agreement to be made, Israel will have to agree to it. This is because an agreement is just that, an agreement between the parties even if they are pressed into it. Why would Israel agree to such a thing? It is because *all nations* are aligned against her. This explains why *all nations* receive horrific punishment but Israel only receives punishment *in measure* because it is *all nations* that carry the greater guilt. If Israel would resist the effort of *all nations* to *devour* her land, there would be no punishment coming her way, as we clearly see next in Zechariah 14. Consider the difference in how God treats Israel in Zechariah 14 verses how He just treated her in Jeremiah 30. This comparison further supports the conclusion that *all nations* in Jeremiah 30 could only *devour* the land through an agreement of some kind and not warfare. Otherwise, as will be shown, it appears God is double-minded.

Jeremiah 30 versus Zechariah 14

In addition to there being no mention of armies going against Israel to *devour,* "plunder," or "seize" the land in Jeremiah 30, we can also support the perspective that it can only be from a *Peace* agreement by comparing the events in Jeremiah 30 to those in Zechariah 14. Consider the contrast between the two. In Zechariah 14 it is clear that *all nations* attempt to remove the land from Israel by force-of-arms in an event that happens much deeper in *the day of the Lord* (end times). In it we are told: *For I will gather <u>all nations</u> against Jerusalem to battle ...* which is clearly an attacking army because they seek a *battle.* In Zechariah 14 the Lord fights against *all nations* whose armies are surrounding and attacking Jerusalem because we are told: *Then shall the* Lord *go forth, and fight against those nations, as when he fought in the day of battle.* This event is part of *the day of the Lord* because in verse 1 we are told: *Behold, the day of the* Lord *cometh ...* indicating it is within *the day of the Lord.* We know it is deep into *the day of the Lord* because it says of Jesus: *And his feet shall stand in that day upon the Mount of Olives...*

Because it is NOT in the beginning but near the end of *the day of the Lord* that Jesus stands on the Mount of Olives, there is no mention of birth pangs anywhere within Zechariah 14. In Zechariah 14 there not only is no punishment against Israel, but the Lord comes against the armies that assaulted her. However, remember we just saw in Jeremiah 30 that *all nations devour* Israel and yet the Lord also punished Israel but *in measure.* Since God is not double minded, there is a good reason for the difference in His responses to the events in Jeremiah 30 versus. Zechariah 14. The difference is that in Jeremiah 30 it is not armies that go against the land of Israel. That leaves only one other way for the land to be devoured, which is a *Peace* agreement that Israel signs on to. Because such an agreement would require Israel to agree to its terms of transferring the land in the name of *Peace,* it brings punishment upon her as well but only *in measure.* Why *in measure?* Because arrayed against Israel on the other side was *all nations,* and God considers what she was up against and gives mercy by only punishing her *in measure.* Therefore, only a *Peace* agreement can *devour* the land in Jeremiah 30.

> **CRITICAL CONCLUSION:** JEREMIAH 30 CONFIRMS IT IS *ALL NA-TIONS* THAT REMOVE LAND FROM ISRAEL WITHOUT WARFARE AND THIS LAUNCHES *THE DAY OF THE LORD*

A Sidebar on Birth Pangs

As a sidebar and in further support of the above conclusion, it is worth noting that Isaiah 34 appears to be describing the same event as that in Zechariah 14. This is further evidence that the birth pangs term is only used for events that transpire during the beginning phase of *the day of the Lord* and, therefore, the term is not used in either Zechariah 14 or Isaiah 34 since both tell of events that occur much later. In Isaiah 34:2 we are told ...

> *For the indignation of the Lord is against all nations. And His fury against all their armies; He has utterly destroyed them...*

Once again we see that the Lord is furious with *all nations* just as He is in Zechariah 14. Also in Isaiah 34 He destroys their armies. Then in Isaiah 34:8 we are told why He has done this:

> *For it is the day of the Lord's vengeance, The year of recompense for the cause of <u>Zion</u>.*

Zion is another word for Jerusalem so the cause for the Lord's wrath against *all nations* in Isaiah 34 is because of what *all nations* have done to Jerusalem. And what they have done is surround it with armies as noted in Zechariah 14, and this time frame within *the day of the Lord* (end times) is referred to as *the year of recompense,* indicating it unfolds over the course of a year but within the broader time frame of *the day of the Lord.* Remember in Zechariah 14 we were told *all nations* were gathered *against Jerusalem to battle* and this caused the Lord to *fight against those nations, as when He fought in the day of battle.* So it is clear that both Zechariah 14 and Isaiah 34 are talking about the armies of *all nations* going against Jerusalem near the end of *the day of the Lord* and the Lord fights against them. In neither

Zechariah 14 nor Isaiah 34 does the Lord punish Israel as the armies of *all nations* come against Jerusalem.

However, in Jeremiah 30 there is no mention of armies going against Israel and she is punished along with *all nations* but *in measure.* Also, in neither Zechariah 14 nor Isaiah 34 is there any birth pangs reference, indicating that the event they are describing does not take place in the beginning phase of *the day of the Lord* (end times). But within Jeremiah 30 there is a birth pangs phrase that places it at the start of *the day of the Lord* and is, therefore, contextually in harmony with what Matthew 24:7-8, 1 Thessalonians 5:1-3, and Joel 3:1-2 are telling us. So Jeremiah 30 is added to the rendition of Scripture indicating that *all nations* will remove land from Israel in an agreement or *covenant* of some kind before the start of *the day of the Lord.*

Harmony: 1 Thessalonians, Joel, and Jeremiah

Remember in 1 Thessalonians 5:2-3 we are told *they* shall proclaim *Peace* before the *sudden destruction* that starts *the day of the Lord.* In Joel 3:2 we are told *all nations* are gathered together by the Lord for punishment because they *parted my land* and this is the reason for the launch of *the day of the Lord.* Because there is no sign that warfare was used to part the land, it leaves a covenant or agreement of some kind as the only other method of accomplishing it. And now Jeremiah 30 is telling us that in the beginning moments of *the day of the Lord,* the Lord makes a *full end* of *all nations* because they *devour* Israel but without any sign of warfare. Here too since warfare is not used to accomplish the devouring of the land it leaves only one other method: a *Peace* agreement. Adding to the case that in Jeremiah 30 it could only be a *Peace* agreement of some kind that removes the land from Israel is the fact that the Jewish state also receives punishment but *in measure.*

Therefore, we see an array of connecting Scriptures that when read literally, using logical inference and within context, speak to it being *all nations* (*they, many, all nations*)who remove land from Israel in the name of *Peace* and that this is the reason for the launch of *the day of the Lord* (end times). Because it is *all nations* that initiate the *covenant* or agreement, this is in harmony with what the prophet Daniel tells us. Consider the clues:

1 Thessalonians 5:3 uses: *they*

Daniel 9:27 uses: *many*

Joel 3:2 uses: *all nations*

Jeremiah 30 uses: *all nations*

Four Warnings Before The End Times Begin

Prophetic Script

1st Rumours of wars for Israel must complete to finish Matthew 24:6. The most likely way for this to be accomplished is an actual war between Israel and Iran, Hamas, and Hezbollah.

2nd (Added this chapter) A notable war (possibly Israel-Iran) that has associated with it some kind of wonders in the heavens. Exactly what these wonders are is not given.

3rd (Added this chapter) The sun shall turn into darkness and the moon into blood (possibly a time of notable solar eclipses and blood moons) before the great war that launches the day of the Lord.

4th Next, All nations initiate an agreement removing land from Israel in the name of Peace.

1st Next The day of the Lord launches with a great war sometime after that Peace agreement initiated by all nations.

2nd The great war between the nations that launches the day of the Lord comes with a thief in the night kind of surprise and includes great earthquakes, famines, pestilences, and thick darkness across the world, making it difficult at times to see the sun, moon, and stars.

3rd (Added this chapter) All nations are severely punished in the beginning of the day of the Lord. Israel is also punished for having agreed to the Peace covenant but only in measure.

CHAPTER FIVE

Daniel: Antichrist Confirms a Previous Covenant With Many (U.N.)

> **Covered in this Chapter:** Another look at the prophet Daniel who confirms it is a multitude of nations (*all nations*) that initiate the peace agreement, which the Antichrist later confirms.

A s mentioned previously, it is Daniel 9:27 that alludes to a *Peace* treaty initiated by *all nations.* Consider again what Daniel had to say concerning an action to be taken by a coming world leader who will be a man of great spiritual darkness. He is known to most people as the Antichrist.

> *And he shall <u>confirm the covenant with many</u> for one week: and in the midst of the week he shall cause the sacrifice and the oblation to cease ... Daniel 9:27*

The action he engages in is that he will *confirm* an agreement relating to Israel for a period of seven years. The big mistake some people make in interpreting this verse is that when they read *confirm* they assume initiate, begin, or start, indicating that the Antichrist will originate that *covenant* or agreement. But that is not what the Scripture is literally telling us. The Hebrew word here for *confirm* is "gabar," which means to "confirm or strengthen." Consider that when you confirm your reservations at a restaurant it is only after a reservation already exists. Or when you seek to strengthen a wall, you are able to do so only after the wall is built. And so it is with a *covenant.* When someone seeks to *confirm* or strengthen a *covenant,* they can only do so after one already exists. What we are being told in this famous verse is that the agreement already exists and this evil leader is the one that will strengthen it or *confirm* it sometime later. And when he does confirm it, this will mark the beginning of his seven year world dominating rule.

Concerning this agreement, or *covenant,* we know from Daniel that it will possess a certain distinct characteristic. This notable characteristic helps to identify it as the one specifically being discussed by the prophet. Daniel describes it as *the covenant with many.* In other words, it is the number of parties involved in this agreement that makes it noteworthy, allowing it to be identified as the one that the Antichrist will eventually *confirm.*

From the multitude of Scriptures we have covered, we know what *covenant* will come into existence, which the Antichrist will later *confirm* for seven years. It is the one spoken of by Jeremiah in chapter 30 in which *all nations devour* the land without any sign of warfare against Israel. It is the same agreement where Joel 3:1-2 tells us *all nations parted* the land also without any sign of warfare against Israel to accomplish it. This causes the Lord to gather *all nations* into the *valley of Jehoshaphat* for the punishment of the great war that launches *the day of the Lord.* Paul tells us in 1 Thessalonians 5:2-3 that the great war comes with *sudden destruction* but only after *they* (in the plural) say *Peace,* telling us Israel is a party to an agreement that must certainly involve removing land from her if it is to be referred to as *Peace.* Paul further alerts us to the fact that this *sudden destruction* comes in the beginning moment of *the day of the Lord* by using the birth pangs term, causing that Scripture to fall in line with events during its beginning time frame, which is consistent with both Joel and Jeremiah. In Matthew 24:7-8, Jesus describes an event as birth pangs wherein *nation shall rise against nation, and kingdom against kingdom,* implying a great multitude of nations going to war that sounds a lot like *all nations.* In agreement with Paul's *sudden destruction,* Jesus tells us the multitudes of nations will suddenly *rise* to war.

As is clear from a multitude of Scripture, it is *all nations* that initiate the agreement or *covenant* described in Daniel 9:27 and then receive their due punishment for removing land that God restored to the Jews in 1948 and 1967. That is why Daniel describes it as *the covenant with many.* Because the word *many* fits perfectly with *all nations* being the ones who initiate it. Sometime after *all nations* initiate this *covenant* the great war that launches *the day of the Lord* arrives and represents punishment against *all nations* for having *parted* the land. Sometime after that war the Antichrist finds himself as the one to *confirm* the initial agreement for a period of seven years.

But there is something else Daniel 9:27 strongly infers. It shows the time frame wherein the transfer of great power to the Antichrist takes place. When considered within the context that *all nations* initiate the *covenant with many,* Daniel 9:27 highlights the time frame wherein a watershed shift in world power in favor of the Antichrist takes place. It is only after that power is transferred that the Antichrist has attained a powerful enough position to be the one to *confirm the covenant with many,* launching his seven year rule.

CRITICAL CONCLUSION: *ALL NATIONS* INITIATE THE *COVE-NANT* THAT ANTICHRIST LATER WILL *CONFIRM*

Prophetic Script

Pre-Birth Pangs Prophetic Time Frame:

1st Rumours of wars for Israel must complete to finish Matthew 24:6. The most likely way for this to be accomplished is an actual war between Israel and Iran, Hamas, and Hezbollah.

Warning # 1 ... Before the "End Times" Launch

2nd (Added this chapter) A notable war (possibly Israel-Iran) that has associated with it some kind of wonders in the heavens. Exactly what these wonders are is not given.

Warning # 2 ... Before the "End Times" Launch

3rd (Added this chapter) The sun shall turn into darkness and the moon into blood (possibly a time of notable solar eclipses and blood moons) before the great war that launches the day of the Lord.

Warning # 3 ... Before the "End Times" Launch

4th Next, All nations initiate an agreement removing land from Israel in the name of Peace.

Birth Pangs Prophetic Time Frame:

1st Next, The day of the Lord launches with a great-war sometime after that Peace agreement initiated by all nations.

2nd The great war between the nations that launches the day of the Lord comes with a thief in the night kind of surprise and includes great earthquakes, famines, pestilences, and thick darkness across the world, making it difficult at times to see the sun, moon, and stars.

3rd All nations are severely punished in the beginning of the day of the Lord. Israel is also punished for having agreed to the Peace covenant but only in measure.

Daniel's 70th Week Prophetic Time Frame:

1st (Added this chapter) Sometime after all nations initiate the Peace covenant removing land from Israel, the Antichrist will confirm it for a period of seven years.

The Rise of the Antichrist

CHAPTER SIX

Revelation 6 & Daniel 9: When World Power Transitions to the Antichrist

Covered in this Chapter: There are two Scriptures in support of the Antichrist rising to power during the birth pangs phase of the day of the Lord.

Covered in this Chapter: The Four Horsemen of the Apocalypse ride during the birth pangs beginning phase of the day of the Lord.

We know from a multitude of Scriptures that sometime after the agreement pushed by *all nations* removing land from Israel, a great war between the nations launches *the day of the Lord* (end times). It is a war that will bring tremendous devastation on a global scale including great *famines, pestilences,* and accompanied by *great earthquakes.* Because in Matthew 24:7 Jesus describes nations and kingdoms rising to war at its beginning, that description appears to be detailing another world war. From history we know that after each previous world war the global power structure was turned upside down. Consider briefly the transformation in the world power structure that took place after World Wars I and II.

After World War I the Ottoman Empire, which had ruled vast portions of the Middle East for centuries, was broken apart and dissolved into the winds of history by the victors of that war. Appearing in its place were dramatically expanded British and French empires that spread out across the entire region. After World War II those same British and French empires immediately began to shrink dramatically altering the global geopolitical picture yet again. However, just as the British and French global empires were shrinking, American and Soviet empires began springing up across the world, eventually developing into a great standoff that was called the Cold War.

Although the political realignments after the first two world wars were great, what should be expected after the great war launching *the day of the Lord* (end times) ought to be even more dramatic. This is because the Scriptures tell us it will be mankind's most terrible and destructive war. This war takes place during the birth pangs phase of *the day of the Lord* described by Jesus as *nation shall rise against nation and kingdom against kingdom.* Since it covers the full spectrum of governmental entities, it implies a large number of nations at war. But during this great war, in addition to a raging world war taking place, mankind will be visited by the additional horrors of terrible *pestilences, famines,* and *great earthquakes in divers places* as mentioned in Matthew 24 and Luke 21. Under such dire conditions, it is difficult to imagine the current world order remaining unchanged. In fact, the Scriptures tell us that a dramatic re-ordering of the world power structure does take place during that great war, within the birth pangs or beginning phase of *the day of the Lord.*

Daniel 9:27 and Revelation 6: The Transition of World Power from All Nations to the Antichrist

---

27 And he shall confirm the covenant with many for one week: and in the midst of the week ... Daniel 9:27

Remember in Daniel 9:27 we determined that the Antichrist actually *confirm[s] the covenant with many,* exactly as the Scripture tells us, instead of initiating it. However, that single verse alerts us to something else that is very significant. It reveals a transition of world power during the birth pangs or beginning phase of *the day of the Lord,* which is characterized by the launch of this great war.

Since a multitude of Scriptures have told us *all nations* will initiate the *Peace* agreement just prior to the great war launching *the day of the Lord,* (end times), it is highly significant and informative that it later becomes the Antichrist who *confirm[s]* that *covenant* for seven years. Therefore, Daniel 9:27 shows a transition in world power during the great war or birth pangs phase of *the day of the Lord.* We see great power possessed by *all nations* prior to the great war that launches *the day of the Lord* and flows to the Antichrist, who is the only one required to *confirm* the initial agreement after the great war. It appears that in the aftermath of the great war Middle East politics are dramatically altered to the point where *all nations* (probably led by the Western powers) are no longer a significant factor there. Since it is no longer *all nations* that must act to *confirm* the agreement they initiated, it is clear that they no longer count as much as Antichrist at that point in time. This demonstrates the transition of power to the Antichrist during the birth pangs phase of *the day of the Lord*. Shortly we will see how Revelation 6 also shows the Antichrist gaining power during the birth pangs time frame, providing our required second Scriptural witness.

So the prophetic time period wherein this transfer of power to the Antichrist takes place is during the birth pangs or beginning phase of *the day of the Lord*. This time frame unfolds just before his terrible seven year rule begins. The moment in time when the Antichrist rises above *all nations* to become the only leader necessary to *confirm the covenant with many* marks the reality of his ascension to power and, therefore, the beginning of his rule. It is at that point in time when he *shall confirm the covenant with many* we are told in Daniel 9:27 his unholy reign will last for exactly seven years.

Revelation 6 Confirms Daniel 9:27 and This Perspective

To confirm the perspective that the Antichrist attains his power during the birth pangs phase of *the day of the Lord* (end times), it is necessary to have a second Scripture come in agreement since we must have two witnesses. That second witness is found in Revelation 6. According to Revelation 6, the Antichrist goes *forth conquering, and to conquer* during the birth pangs phase of *the day of the Lord*. How do we know Revelation 6 is describing the birth pangs or beginning phase of *the day of the Lord?* Because much of what is described in Revelation 6 matches Jesus' description given in Matthew 24:7 of the events that represent the *beginning of sorrows* which He describes as birth pangs, we also see that prior to Revelation 6 there is no indication within the five previous Revelation chapters of any horrific events striking the world or any sign that *the day of the Lord* has yet begun. This too is in harmony with the birth pangs *beginning,* described by Jesus in Matthew 24:7. By establishing that Revelation 6 unfolds within the birth pangs phase of *the day of the Lord,* it confirms that the Antichrist makes his move for power during that prophetic phase, which is marked by mankind's greatest war up to that point in history. Remember the proper context here. In Daniel 9:27, it is no longer *all nations* but the Antichrist alone who is required to *confirm the covenant with many* after the birth pangs phase has ended, even though it was *all nations* that originally initiated the *covenant.*

Revelation 6 Shows How Power Transitions to the Antichrist

In the Book of Revelation chapters 1 through 5, there are no signs that *the day of the Lord* (end times) has yet begun. There is no mention of the wars, *famines, pestilences,* or *earthquakes* given to us by Jesus in Matthew 24:7-8 as the beginning signs to look for. It is not until Revelation 6 that the beginning moment of *the day of the Lord* appears in stark detail. There are six seals out of a total of seven opened by the hand of Jesus in Revelation 6 and all but one tells a cataclysmic story. As previously noted, the rendition of those beginning events in Revelation 6 match the description Jesus provides in Matthew 24:7. Shortly we will look at a comparison to establish this. But first consider the opening two verses in Revelation 6 and their demonstration of how power is attained by the Antichrist during the great war that launches the birth pangs phase.

> *¹And I saw when the Lamb opened one of the seals, and I heard, as it were the noise of thunder, one of the four beasts saying, Come and see.*

> *² And I saw, and behold a white horse: and he that sat on him had a bow; and a crown was given unto him: and he went forth conquering, and to conquer. Revelation 6:1-2*

This first seal unleashes the *white horse* and he who rides it receives a *crown* then *he went forth conquering, and to conquer.* This character on the *white horse* is the Antichrist conducting himself as a counterfeit Christ going about establishing his kingdom through warfare. How do we know this rider on the *white horse* is Antichrist and not Jesus in Revelation 6? Because later in Revelation 19, the true Christ appears on a *white horse* and the difference between the two is significant as noted by comparing the following verses.

> *¹¹ And I saw heaven opened, and behold a white horse; and he that sat upon him was called Faithful and True, and in righteousness he doth judge and make war. Revelation 19:11*

Here is Jesus on a *white horse* and He is *called Faithful and True.* However, in Revelation 6 the one who rides that *white horse* is given no such title.

> *¹² His eyes were as a flame of fire, and on his head were many crowns; and he had a name written, that no man knew, but he himself. Revelation 19:12*

The character in Revelation 6 has a *crown* given to him. But the real Jesus already has *many crowns.*

> *[13] And he was clothed with a vesture dipped in blood: and his name is called The Word of God. [14]And the armies which were in heaven followed him upon white horses, clothed in fine linen, white and clean. Revelation 19:13-14*

Here we see that the true Jesus has an entourage made up of the *armies which are in heaven* following him on *white horses.* But the impostor in Revelation 6 rides by himself. The true Jesus is noted here for *a vesture dipped in blood,* signifying his sacrificial death. However, the rider of the *white horse* in Revelation 6 is granted no such honor.

> *[15] And out of his mouth goeth a sharp sword, that with it he should smite the nations: and he shall rule them with a rod of iron: and he treadeth the winepress of the fierceness and wrath of Almighty God.*

The real Jesus carries a *sharp sword* and also uses a *rod of iron* but in Revelation 6 the impostor carries a *bow.*

Since the differences between the riders of the *white horse* in Revelation 6 compared to Revelation 19 are so great, they cannot be describing the same individual. Yet it is abundantly clear the rider in Revelation 19 is Jesus. Therefore, the rider in Revelation 6 cannot be Jesus, which leaves the Antichrist as the only other possibility. Understanding that the rider of the *white horse* in Revelation 6 is the Antichrist, we see that he is going *forth conquering* during the great war that launches the birth pangs phase of *the day of the Lord* (end times). In line with what we saw in Daniel 9:27, a transfer of power from *all nations* to the Antichrist, during that birth pangs great war as well. It is only after he has completed his conquest during the chaos of the birth pangs time frame that Daniel 9:27 tells us the Antichrist becomes the one to *confirm the covenant* that *all nations* had previously initiated. Remember, Daniel describes the agreement that the Antichrist will *confirm* as *the covenant with many* another way of describing *all nations* who initiated it. Now we will establish that Revelation 6 is, in fact, a description of the birth pangs phase of *the day of the Lord* by comparing the description of its events to those given by Jesus in Matthew 24:7,which He described as the *beginning of sorrows* and used the term birth pangs.

The second, third, fourth, and sixth seals of Revelation 6 match the events Jesus provides in Matthew 24:7 as *the beginning of sorrows.* The second seal unleashes a red horse that takes *peace from the earth, and that they should kill one another: and there was given unto him a great sword.* That matches the great war Jesus describes in Matthew 24:7, where *nation shall rise against nation.*

The third seal brings out a *black horse; and he that sat on him had a pair of balances in his hand.* *⁶And I heard a voice in the midst of the four beasts say, A measure of wheat for a penny, and three measures of barley for a penny; and see thou hurt not the oil and the wine.* This is describing either *famines,* great inflation, or both.

After the fourth seal is opened, there appears a *pale horse* and after the verse reiterates a rendition of war and hunger, then it is indicated that *the beasts of the earth* would join them in afflicting mankind. It should be noted that there is no greater *beasts of the earth* than disease. It is not reasonable to believe this is referring to lions, tigers, and bears attacking people all over the earth. This then describes the same *pestilences* also provided in Jesus' rendition in Matthew 24:7. This fourth seal completes the four horsemen of Revelation. But the seals continue to be opened.

The fifth seal speaks to the condition of *the souls of them that were slain for the word of God, and for the testimony which they held* who are impatiently waiting for God to avenge their blood. Then the sixth seal:

> *¹²And I beheld when he had opened the sixth seal ,and, lo, there was a great earthquake; and the sun became black as sackcloth of hair, and the moon became as blood; ¹³And the stars of heaven fell unto the earth, even as a fig tree casteth her untimely figs, when she is shaken of a mighty wind.*

After adding additional information compared to Matthew 24:7, this Scripture also refers to *earthquakes.*

Now consider Matthew 24:7 and Revelation 6 side by side.

Matthew 24:7	Revelation 6
Great War	2nd Seal: Great War
Famine	3rd Seal: Famine
Pestilence	4th Seal: Wars, Pestilence, and Famine
Earthquakes	6th Seal: Great Earthquake & More Details

Although Matthew 24:7 does not include the impact on the *sun, moon,* and *stars* during *the day of the Lord,* other Scriptures we have previously covered do. As previously noted, it is <u>before</u> *the day of the Lord* that only the *sun* and *moon* are impacted. However, it is <u>during</u> *the day of the Lord* that the *sun, moon,* and *stars* are impacted, which is in line with how the *sixth seal* is described.

If there is any doubt remaining that the events described in Revelation 6 unfold during the birth pangs phase of *the day of the Lord* (end times), those doubts are dispelled by that chapter's final two verses.

---

[16] And said to the mountains and rocks, Fall on us, and hide us from the face of him that sitteth on the throne, and from the wrath of the Lamb:

---

[17] For the great day of his wrath is come; and who shall be able to stand?

The term *the great day of his wrath* refers to the wrath of God on the multitudes of sinners. It is the day of God's wrath, which is also referred to as *the day of the Lord.* We are being told the events being described in Revelation 6 are part of *the day of the Lord.* It is important to note that nowhere in the previous five chapters in Revelation is there any mention of *the day of the Lord* or a phrase that represents it. Also, nowhere in the previous five chapters in Revelation is there any sign of destructive events. Only in Revelation 6 does it first appear, along with the description of events almost identical to those mentioned in Matthew 24:7 as the *beginning of sorrows* ... birth pangs.

The Structure of the book of Revelation Confirms the Birth Pangs Beginning Time Frame

It is worth reiterating here that it is no coincidence the first six seals opened within Revelation 6 are separate from all other cataclysmic events described in the remaining chapters of Revelation. Consider their separate nature and the fact that all horrific events within the Book of Revelation flow from seven seals that are opened in heaven.

It is from heaven that those seven seals are opened by Jesus and unleash the wrath of God on the earth including the Four Horsemen of the apocalypse. However, Revelation 6 clearly demarcates the first six seals from the *seventh seal* opened later in chapter 8. And those first six seals match the details Jesus gives us of the beginning of *the day of the Lord,* telling us *the great day of his wrath is come,* indicating it has started. However, the seventh seal is separated from those first six seals and opened, by itself in chapter 8. And when the *seventh seal* is opened it literally unleashes all remaining horrific events foretold in the Book of Revelation including the seven *trumpet* judgments and the seven *bowl* judgments.

That *seventh seal* is clearly separate from the first six seals as made clear by the fact it is opened in chapter 8. This separation of the first six seals from the seventh is not by chance. Rather, it lines up with the effort of Jesus in Matthew 24:6-8 and Paul in 1 Thessalonians 5:1-3 wherein they use a birth pangs term to demarcate the beginning phase to *the day of the Lord.* This demarcation for seal seven from the first six seals makes it clear that they are prophetically separate from the seventh seal. And this is because they take place within the beginning phase of *the day of the Lord.* Remember, near the end of chapter 6, we are told the events contained within the chapter are *the wrath of the Lamb,* and this is the first place in Revelation that we see the wrath of God. In other words, it is the beginning of His wrath. And the beginning of the wrath of God is, of course, the beginning of *the day of the Lord,* which we know is described by Jesus, Paul, and Jeremiah as birth pangs. This division of seals in the Book of Revelation confirms the separate nature of the birth pangs phase of *the day of the Lord.*

It is clear that Revelation 6 is relaying the same events given to us by Jesus in Matthew 24:7, where those events are described as the *beginning of sorrows.* This means that the *white horse* described in Revelation 6 rides during the birth pangs prophetic phase of *the day of the Lord* just as previously indicated. Therefore we are being shown that the *white horse* in the first seal is the Antichrist establishing his unholy empire by going *forth conquering, and to conquer* during the birth pangs prophetic time frame and he is obviously very successful. We know he is very successful because we understand from Daniel 9:27 that after the great war that launches the birth pangs time frame he has risen above *all nations* to become the only one required to *confirm the covenant with many* that *all nations* had previously initiated. We can deduct that at the point in time wherein he *confirm[s] the covenant with many,* the great war is over because he is now a significant world leader. This is because if that war was still raging, it would be unreasonable to think he would be positioned to *confirm* an agreement since his rise to power would be contested.

CRITICAL CONCLUSION: THE ANTICHRIST RISES TO POWER DURING THE BIRTH PANGS PHASE OF *THE DAY OF THE LORD* AFTER POWER TRANSFERRED FROM *ALL NATIONS*

Prophetic Script

Pre-Birth Pangs Prophetic Time Frame:

1st Rumours of wars for Israel must complete to finish Matthew 24:6. The most likely way for this to be accomplished is an actual war between Israel and Iran, Hamas, and Hezbollah.

Warning # 1 ... Before the "End Times" Launch

2nd (Added this chapter) A notable war (possibly Israel-Iran) that has associated with it some kind of wonders in the heavens. Exactly what these wonders are is not given.

Warning # 2 ... Before the "End Times" Launch

3rd (Added this chapter) The sun shall turn into darkness and the moon into blood (possibly a time of notable solar eclipses and blood moons) before the great war that launches the day of the Lord.

Warning # 3 ... Before the "End Times" Launch

4th Next, All nations initiate an agreement removing land from Israel in the name of Peace.

Birth Pangs Prophetic Time Frame:

1st Next, The day of the Lord launches with a great war sometime after that Peace agreement initiated by all nations.

2nd The great war between the nations that launches the day of the Lord comes with a thief in the night kind of surprise and includes great earthquakes, famines, pestilences, and thick darkness across the world, making it difficult at times to see the sun, moon, and stars.

3rd All nations are severely punished in the beginning of the day of the Lord. Israel is also punished for having agreed to the Peace covenant but only in measure.

4th (Added this chapter) The time frame wherein the Antichrist rises to power is the birth pangs beginning phase of the day of the Lord.

5th (Added this chapter) The Four Horsemen of the Apocalypse start riding during the birth pangs beginning phase of the day of the Lord.

Daniel's 70th Week Prophetic Time Frame:

1st Sometime after all nations initiate the Peace covenant removing land from Israel, the Antichrist will confirm it for a period of seven years. This begins Daniel's 70th Week

CHAPTER SEVEN

Time Frames: The Antichrist Kingdom *versus* The Day of the Lord

The Length of the Antichrist Rule

There are numerous Scriptures which tell us that the Antichrist kingdom will last for a period of seven years. We see those seven years mentioned in Daniel 9:27 wherein we are told *he shall confirm the covenant with many for one week: and in the midst of the week he shall cause the sacrifice and the oblation to cease* ... This Scripture tells us that after the Antichrist becomes the one to *confirm the covenant with many* previously initiated by *all nations* that in the *midst* (middle) of the seven years he will begin causing great trouble for the Jews. It is during the second half of the seven years that he begins interfering with their utilization of the rebuilt temple by preventing them from offering sacrifices to God. Although this Scripture identifies how long the rule of the Antichrist will last, it makes no mention of how long *the day of the Lord* is.

Daniel 7:25 adds its weight to the Antichrist kingdom lasting seven 7 years by stressing the great difficulties faced during the last 3½ years of his rule by mentioning that the Jews and remaining Christians *shall be given into his* [Antichrist's] *hand until a time and times and the dividing of time.* In plain English that is 3½ years. Daniel 12:7 also mentions those last 3½ years noting that *the power of holy people* will be scattered during that time. In Revelation 11:2-3 we are told *the holy city will be tread under foot forty and two months* and that during that time God will send two witnesses to Jerusalem who will prophecy *a thousand two hundred and threescore days.* Using the Hebrew 360-day calendar, that is 3½ years as well. There are other verses that reference those 3 ½ years representing the final half of the Antichrist's rule as being a horrific time. However, none of these Scriptures refer to the length of *the day of the Lord* but only the length of the Antichrist's rule.

As previously covered in chapter two concerning *the day of the Lord,* we know from Jesus and Paul that it launches at the precise beginning of what is popularly referred to as the end times. From Zechariah and Isaiah we know it continues until Jesus sets foot on the Mount of Olives, which is years later. So we know *the day of the Lord* is measured in multiple years. Only in Isaiah 34 do we find a Scripture that mentions a length of time while discussing *the day of the Lord.* However, what Isaiah 34 does is simply demarcate a year within the broader time frame (multiple years) of *the day of the Lord* describing it as *the year of recompences for the controversy of Zion.* Isaiah 34 appears to be describing the same event as Zechariah 14 wherein armies are surrounding Jerusalem. And then it applies the term *the year of recompences for the controversy of Zion* because that one year within the broader time frame of *the day of the Lord* is focused on Jerusalem. So we are still without any clear Scriptural reference as to the exact length of *the day of the Lord.* But, we do know it is measured in multiple years.

The conclusion that *the day of the Lord* is measured in years is derived by reading the Scriptures as literally as possible and applying reason and common sense to them. It is only the traditions of men that say the "end times" last exactly seven years by assuming the length of the Antichrist's rule as the full length of the "end times." However, *the day of the Lord* is the "end times" and reading the Scriptures literally, we see it is divided into two distinct time frames. There is the beginning phase, referred to as birth pangs, which accounts for the rise of the Antichrist placing him in position to *confirm the covenant with many* that *all nations* had previously initiated. This birth pangs prophetic time frame is separated from the rest of *the day of the Lord* by Jesus Christ and the prophets Paul, Jeremiah, and Isaiah. We also see that the structure of Revelation 6 speaks to this division of *the day of the Lord.* In Revelation 6, we see in seals 2, 3, 4, and 6 the same events described by Jesus in Matthew 24:7 as birth pangs. Thereafter in Revelation 8 the seventh seal is finally broken, unleashing all 14 remaining cataclysms in the book and indicating a clear demarcation between the birth pangs events in chapter 6 and everything else.

> CRITICAL CONCLUSION: THE DAY OF THE LORD ENCOMPASS-
> ES THE BIRTH PANGS BEGINNING PHASE AND THE ANTICHRIST'S
> SEVEN-YEAR RULE.

By identifying Revelation 6 as occurring in the beginning moments of *the day of the Lord,* and its rider of the *white horse* as the Antichrist, it confirms that it is during the birth pangs or beginning phase of *the day of the Lord* that the Antichrist rises to power by *conquering, and to conquer.* Thereafter, it is he alone who commands the most powerful perch in the world and is the only leader required to *confirm the covenant with many* that Daniel spoke about in 9:27. It is at that moment and not before that his ungodly seven-year rule begins. It is also at the moment when he *confirms the covenant* that the birth pangs phase of *the day of the Lord* is completed, leaving the final seven years to unfold. However, the seven-year time frame of the Antichrist's rule also represents the final and dramatic ending to another prophecy given by Daniel and referred to as the "70ᵗʰ week" prophecy.

Birth Pangs Phase Announces the Impending Birth of Daniel's 70th Week

In the Book of Daniel we are given a prophecy in chapter 9 verses 24-27 that provides a panoramic view of God's plan for mankind. It includes Jesus' death on the cross then goes all the way until His return. Because it is a major end time prophecy, it must be addressed here briefly with our interest in it limited to the last verse.

---

²⁴ *Seventy weeks are determined upon thy people and upon thy holy city, to finish the transgression, and to make an end of sins, and to make reconciliation for iniquity, and to bring in everlasting righteousness, and to seal up the vision and prophecy, and to anoint the most Holy. (The culmination of God's salvation plan will take place over a period of 70 weeks of years or 490 Hebrew years.)*

---

²⁵ *Know therefore and understand, that from the going forth of the commandment to restore and to build Jerusalem unto the Messiah the Prince shall be seven weeks, and threescore and two weeks: the street shall be built again, and the wall, even in troublous times. (This is a literal and specifically accurate prophecy identifying the year of the completion of Jesus' mission of salvation on the cross. This verse covers the first 69 weeks of years. "seven weeks, and threescore and two weeks.")*

> ^{26} And after threescore and two weeks shall Messiah be cut off, but not for himself: and the people of the prince that shall come shall destroy the city and the sanctuary; and the end thereof shall be with a flood, and unto the end of the war desolations are determined. (This prophecy acknowledges the death of the Messiah in 32 A.D. and the later destruction of the Jewish Temple in the year 70 A.D.)

At this point with only 69 weeks accounted for, Daniel's prophecy still has the final or, 70th week, which is now our focus. That final week of years is accounted for in the following verse we have previously looked at, but now, consider it again but from a different perspective.

> ^{27} And he shall confirm the covenant with many for one week: and in the midst of the week he shall cause the sacrifice and the oblation to cease, and for the overspreading of abominations he shall make it desolate, even until the consummation, and that determined shall be poured upon the desolate.

The perspective here is that the birth pangs prophetic time period which demarcates the beginning part of *the day of the Lord* from its later events is a de facto announcement of the impending birth of Daniel's 70th and final week. This is why Jesus, Paul, Isaiah, and Jeremiah all refer to it as birth pangs. It is after the culmination of the difficult birth pangs phase the 70th week of Daniel is birthed the moment the Antichrist *confirm[s] the covenant with many for one week.* So the term birth pangs is used to indicate the approaching birth of Daniel's 70th week. At the end of Daniel's 70th week, Jesus Christ returns to the earth. Amen!

The following is what results from this very literal perspective on prophecy Scriptures. It is not in line with the generally accepted belief that the end times last a total of seven-years only.

	1st	2nd
Prophetic Time Frame:	Birth Pangs	The Antichrist rule
Length:	?	7 years (70th week of Daniel)
Major Events:	Great War wherein The Antichrist gains power 4 Horsemen of Apocalypse ride	The Antichrist rules earth & defiles new Jewish temple
Prophetic Meaning:	Announcing the impending birth of Daniel's 70th week	The end result is Jesus' Second coming

If you disagree with this breakdown, then here is a challenge. Try to find in the Scriptures an indication of how long *the day of the Lord* is. You may want to try for seven-years. Or you may want to try for one year. Or, as is indicated by an array of Scriptures presented here, you may want to accept that *the day of the Lord* encompasses everything we call the end times and must be greater than seven-years. It is within the broader prophetic time frame of *the day of the Lord* where the much touted seven-year prophetic time frame of the Antichrist rule is the 70th week of Daniel. But, clearly the horrific birth pangs happen before his rule begins and act as a de facto announcement of the impending birth of the 70th week.

> **CRITICAL CONCLUSION:** THE BIRTH PANGS TIME FRAME OF *THE DAY OF THE LORD* IS A DE FACTO ANNOUNCMENT THAT DANIEL'S 70TH WEEK IS ABOUT TO BE BORN.

Prophetic Script

Pre-Birth Pangs Prophetic Time Frame:

1st Rumours of wars for Israel must complete to finish Matthew 24:6. The most likely way for this to be accomplished is an actual war between Israel and Iran, Hamas, and Hezbollah.

2nd (Added this chapter) A notable war (possibly Israel-Iran) that has associated with it some kind of wonders in the heavens. Exactly what these wonders are is not given.

3rd (Added this chapter) The sun shall turn into darkness and the moon into blood (possibly a time of notable solar eclipses and blood moons) before the great war that launches the day of the Lord.

4th Next, All nations initiate an agreement removing land from Israel in the name of Peace.

1st Next, The day of the Lord launches with a great war sometime after that Peace agreement initiated by all nations.

2nd The great war between the nations that launches the day of the Lord comes with a thief in the night kind of surprise and includes great earthquakes, famines, pestilences, and thick darkness across the world, making it difficult at times to see the sun, moon, and stars.

3rd All nations are severely punished in the beginning of the day of the Lord. Israel is also punished for having agreed to the Peace covenant but only in measure.

4th The time frame wherein the Antichrist rises to power is the birth pangs beginning phase of the day of the Lord.

5th The Four Horsemen of the Apocalypse start riding during the birth pangs beginning phase of the day of the Lord.

1st Sometime after all nations initiate the Peace covenant removing land from Israel, the Antichrist will confirm it for a period of seven-years. This begins Daniel's 70th Week.

2nd (Added this chapter) The shift of world power to the Antichrist during the birth pangs phase is completed at the moment he is the one to confirm the covenant with many that all nations initiated. That moment launches his seven-year rule and the 70th week of Daniel.

CHAPTER EIGHT

How the Jewish Temple Gets Built

> **Covered in this Chapter:** It is likely that the Antichrist will rise out of a Middle Eastern empire.
>
> **Covered in this Chapter:** The initial peace agreement by *all nations* does not need to be for seven-years nor allow the temple to be rebuilt at the time it is consummated. It only needs to establish *the covenant with many* later to be confirmed by the Antichrist for seven-years.

There is something else the Antichrist will be noted for doing according to 2 Thessalonians 2:3-4. In speaking about him, we are told he is the one ...

Who opposeth and exalteth himself above all that is called God, or that is worshipped; so <u>that he as God sitteth in the temple of God</u>, shewing himself that he is God.

This passage starts by giving a glimpse into the character of this unholy man. He *opposeth* God and will *exalteth himself above all that is called God.* Then he does a very specific act, *He as God sitteth in the temple of God, shewing himself that he is God.* This is the Antichrist at his worst, sitting in the Jewish Holy of Holies temple and proclaiming himself to be a god in a great insult directed against the true God. That temple is the one that historically stood on the Temple Mount in East Jerusalem. That last temple was completely destroyed by the Romans in the year 70 A.D. However, this sacrilegious action on the part of the Antichrist begs the following question. How can this prophecy be completed since there is no Jewish temple currently sitting on the Temple Mount?

It is clear that in order for this prophecy to be fulfilled there must first be a new Jewish temple constructed on the Temple Mount, which the Antichrist can then defile. But how does the temple get there? Those who believe the Antichrist initiates *the covenant with many* instead of *confirm* it must take the position that the initial agreement involving Israel will allow them a portion of the Temple Mount, whereon they can then begin building their new temple. However, when it is understood that *all nations* (United Nations) initiates the agreement resulting in Daniel's *covenant with many,* there is no need for the initial agreement to include Jewish rights to a portion of the Temple Mount. This is because there is still the moment wherein the Antichrist will *confirm* the agreement. But all of this leads to another question.

What are the chances that within the initial *Peace* agreement by *all nations* (United Nations) that a portion of the Temple Mount will be given to the Jews so they can rebuild their temple on it? The answer to that question is that the odds are zero and this is why. For the United Nations to agree upon a *Peace* settlement between the Israelis and Palestinians, there must not be contained within it any element that is completely unacceptable to Muslims. This means that if so much as one square foot of the Temple Mount is given to Israel within a U.N. *Peace* agreement, no Muslim will ever agree to it. The reason for this is quite simple. Upon the Temple Mount sits Islam's third holiest shrine Al–Aqsa Mosque, known to Westerners as the Dome of the Rock. Therefore, the entire Muslim world will be ferociously opposed to giving the Jews any part of the Temple Mount. How intense are Muslim feelings about this? Consider what happened in June of 1967.

After Israel completely and thoroughly defeated the combined armies of Egypt, Jordan, and Syria in a war that lasted only six days, she suddenly became the supreme military might in her neighborhood. Captured within that war was East Jerusalem and with it the Temple Mount. The moment in which the Jews retook the Temple Mount represented the first time since 70 A.D. that they had control over their most holy grounds. Being at the zenith of her power, Israel could have done anything with the Temple Mount she chose and no one could stop her. But what did she choose to do? Israel immediately returned it back to the control of the Muslim religious leaders who had previously overseen it. Why would Israel do such a thing after waiting almost 1,900 years to regain control over it? Because she knew any effort to retain that control would incite non-stop attacks from every Muslim nation in the world. Now consider what happened when an Israeli leader dared to step foot on the Temple Mount in the year 2000.

When Israeli opposition leader Ariel Sharon led a small delegation to the Temple Mount in September 2000, in a statement of Jewish desire toward the holy site the response from Muslims was immediate and swift. Sharon's action was met by an immediate launching by Muslims of the Second Intifada, also known as the Al-Aqsa Intifada, named after the Muslim holy site located there. The end result was 3,000 Palestinian and 1,000 Israeli deaths before the firestorm settled down. And all of that was a reaction to an Israeli leader simply stepping foot on the

Mount. Now try to imagine the entire Muslim world's response to an effort within the United Nations to permanently give Israel a portion of the Temple Mount so they can build a Jewish temple on it.

If *all nations* (the U.N.) attempt to include Jewish rights to a portion of the Temple Mount in the initial *Peace* agreement, every Muslim nation would oppose it. Additionally they would bring along all of their General Assembly and Security Council allies in a deluge of no votes. Any promotion of a Jewish temple to be built on their holy grounds within a *Peace* agreement will produce a general rage within the Muslim community across the entire world that will be apoplectic even by their standards. It should also be noted that spiritually the United Nations is of the world, and the world is pulling away from the Jews and moving toward the Muslims. So there is no possibility that the initial United Nations (*all nations*) agreement of *Peace* between the Israelis and Palestinians can include any Jewish rights to rebuild their temple on the Temple Mount. This political reality, along with a literal reading of Daniel 9:27, defuses the notion that the initial *Peace* agreement will enable the Jews to rebuild their temple. Daniel 9:27 alerts us that there is no need for that right to be contained within it once it is understood that *all nations* initiate the agreement and not the Antichrist. This is because there is still the moment wherein the Antichrist will sometime later *confirm* it for seven-years.

Once we understand the impossibility of the United Nations (*all nations*) to grant the Jews the right to rebuild their temple on the Temple Mount, we know it can only be approved later when the initial agreement is confirmed by the Antichrist. That raises another question. How does the Antichrist get past the extreme Muslim opposition to the Jews rebuilding their temple on the Temple Mount? Considering the fierce Muslim reaction to a Jewish leader stepping foot on the mount simple logic and reason tell us the idea of the Jews erecting a temple on a large portion of it will take a leader who the Muslims will obey without question. So the best answer to that problem is that the Antichrist has to possess unprecedented political and religious authority over all Muslims. His political and religious authority must be unmatched and unquestioned to pull this off.

We know from Daniel 9:27 and Revelation 6 that the Antichrist will consolidate his power during the beginning (birth pangs) of *the day of the Lord,* and only later will he *confirm the covenant with many* and this indicates the completion of his rise to world power. However, there are some very specific details relating to him that are revealed in the Book of Revelation that provide clues as to why he is able to get the Jewish temple rebuilt. In Revelation 17:12-13, the Antichrist appears to possess unquestioned even the slavish loyalty and authority over the leaders of ten kingdoms. However, these leaders are not your typical kings. They appear to exist for only a very short period of time and only to give him power by willingly turning over the keys of their kingdoms to him. It is the strangest rise of an empire in history. But within this verse are enough clues to make an educated guess as to what current day entities will eventually be involved in the formation of the Antichrist kingdom.

A Strange and Unusual Consolidation of Power

We are told in Revelation 17 that not just one, but ten leaders will turn over their power and kingdoms to the Antichrist. This same group of ten is also mentioned in Revelation 13:1, where we are told the Antichrist kingdom will consist of *ten horns, and upon the horns ten crowns.* The prophet Daniel described the Antichrist kingdom as being *diverse from all the beasts that were before it; and it had ten horns.* It is Revelation 17:12-13 that also refers to the same *ten* but adds some significant details.

And the ten horns which thou sawest are ten kings, which have received no kingdom as yet; but receive power as kings one hour with the beast. These have one mind, and shall give their power and strength unto the beast.

What this verse literally appears to be saying is this: There are *ten kings* who are without any real power. Then they receive power with the Antichrist but for only a very short time. Being of *one mind* they then give him all of their power. Now let's add another Scripture.

O Assyrian, the rod of mine anger, and the staff in their hand is mine indignation. Isaiah 10:5

The context of this verse in Isaiah is the end times and the person being referred to as the *Assyrian* is the Antichrist. So in it we see that the Antichrist is referred to by the area of the world where he comes from, just as Jesus was referred to as the Nazarene. Assyria is an area of the Middle East. Since the overwhelming masses of Middle Easterners are Muslim, that makes the odds of the Antichrist being a Muslim close to 100%. And this conclusion makes the most sense within the mindset that he would have to be a Muslim to pull off allowing the Jews to rebuild their temple. But simply being a Muslim would not be enough to accomplish such a feat. He would also have to possess great religious authority over all Muslims. Now consider what the Scriptures say pertaining to how he presents himself and is received by his followers.

For thou hast said in thine heart, I will ascend into heaven, I will exalt my throne above the stars of God: ... I will be like the most High. Isaiah 14:13-14

... he shall exalt himself, and magnify himself above every god ... Daniel 11:36

Who opposeth and exalteth himself above all that is called God, or that is worshipped; so that he as God sitteth in the temple of God, shewing himself that he is God. 2 Thessalonians 2:4

As these Scriptures indicate, he is presented and presents himself as a god. So he is a Muslim that presents himself and is treated like a god and who is not prevented by the Muslim masses from granting a part of the Temple Mount to the Jews for them to rebuild their temple. There is only one person that the Muslims would respond to like that and it is their much-awaited Islamic savior the Mahdi. It is only the Muslim Mahdi in whom Muslim leaders would *have one mind* in slavish devotion just as Revelation 17 says will exist. There is no other leader that could rise up on the earth that could produce that kind of loyalty. Since all Muslims are eagerly awaiting the Mahdi they will *have one mind* of loyalty toward him.

Presently, Middle Eastern conflicts are dominated by those who *have one mind* toward an expressed goal. They are the four main terrorist groups also responsible for the massive persecution of Christians across the region. These groups go by the names ISIS, Al-Qa'ida, al-Shabab, and Boko Haram, all of whom have taken large tracts of land from nation-states across the region. All of these groups fight, persecute, and kill for a single goal: the formation of an Islamic Caliphate across the Middle East. They *have one mind* and are growing in power. Each one is the spawned offspring of the Muslim Brotherhood, the mother ship of Islamic terrorism in the region and also a fervent proponent of a revived Islamic Caliphate. All of them are of *one mind* toward this goal!

A Muslim Antichrist appears to fit well within the paradigm of Islamic eschatology as well. Consider what Muslim end time prophecy says about the rider of the *white horse* in Revelation 6. And remember that within the perspective presented in this book, the rider of the *white horse* in Revelation 6 is the Antichrist rising to power. According to author and speaker Joel Richardson in his book, *Antichrist: Islam's Awaited Messiah*, Muslim theologians accept that the rider on the *white horse* in Revelation 6 is a representation of their much-awaited al-Mahdi, or christ. Richardson concludes that the Islamic view is that "The Mahdi is believed to ride a white horse." Also quoted within his book are two Egyptian Islamic authors who also claim the Mahdi is found in the Book of Revelation chapter 6. According to Richardson the two well-known Egyptian writers, Muhammad Ibn 'Izzat and Muhammad Arif in their book *Al Mahdi, and the End of Time*, quote Muslim scholar Ka'b al-Ahbar as saying:

I find the Mahdi in the Book of the Prophets ... for instance, the Book of Revelation says: "And I saw behold a white horse. He that sat on it went forth conquering and to conquer."

Understanding that the Antichrist will likely be the Muslim Mahdi resolves three significant prophetic questions. First it explains how Islamic objections to the Jews rebuilding their temple are overcome. It is only the Islamic Mahdi who could overcome those objections, thus allowing the Jews to rebuild their temple next to Islam's third most holy site. There is no other individual or international organization that 1.6 billion Muslims would listen to on the matter since it is only toward their Mahdi that they will *have one mind* in obedience. This can only happen after he comes into world power, which happens during the great war or birth pangs phase of *the day of the Lord.* Once that great power is attained, it should become apparent to the Muslim masses that he is their Mahdi, which explains why it is only after that war he is strong enough to *confirm the covenant with many.*

Secondly, an Islamic Antichrist also explains why at the time when the *covenant with many* is confirmed there will be a provision allowing the Jews to rebuild their temple on the Temple Mount. It is so that he, as a Muslim, can defile the Jewish temple after it is completed. This desire to defile it not only explains why he will insist that the Jews rebuild it at the time he has ascended above *all nations,* but it also answers a third question. It explains why the second half of his seven-year rule is so much worse than the first half. It is because during the first 3½ years of his rule he must consolidate the power he amassed as he went about *conquering* during the great war, which launches the birth pangs beginning phase of *the day of the Lord.* He must also restrain himself from persecuting the Jews prior to their completing and dedicating the new temple to the Lord. It is only after the Jews complete and dedicate the new temple that the Antichrist will be able to ... *As God sitteth in the temple of God, shewing himself that he is God.* Thereafter begins the horrific second half of his seven-year rule, including his brutal scattering of the Jews for their last time. But in order to properly defile the Jewish temple he must have the Jews, of their own free will and by their own hands complete it and then dedicate it to the Lord. He knows if he allows his true nature to be revealed before it is completed they will not finish the job. This logic indicates that its rebuilding and dedication will take about 3 years from the time he *confirm[s] the covenant with many*.

A Final Point

Since the Antichrist will *confirm the covenant with many* for seven-years that does not tell us how long the initial agreement produced by *all nations* will be. But obviously that agreement does not have to be for seven-years. It is important to understand that when *all nations* accomplish the initial agreement, removing a portion of the land from Israel, it does not need to be for seven-years. It also does not need to allow the Jewish temple to be rebuilt on the Temple Mount at that point in time. This needs to be stressed because many Bible prophecy students are waiting for an initial seven-year agreement that allows the Jewish temple to be rebuilt on the Temple Mount. Once that is done, they will then seek to identify the main world leader promoting it as the Antichrist. However, that line of thinking represents significant confusion based on what the multitude of Scriptures we have covered are indicating. Those embracing that belief will be surprised when the coming *Peace* agreement is consummated by *all nations,* does not allocate a portion of the Temple Mount for the Jews, is probably not for seven-years, and no real leader can be segregated out of the process to attach the label of Antichrist to. Many will be confused and completely miss the significance of the moment. So it is important to understand that the only Scriptural requirement of the initial agreement is that it removes land from Israel and that *all nations* initiate it so it represents a *covenant with many.* That is all!

> CRITICAL CONCLUSION: THE PEACE AGREEMENT INITIATED BY *ALL NATIONS* DOES NOT HAVE TO BE FOR SEVEN-YEARS OR ALLOW THE TEMPLE TO BE REBUILT.

Prophetic Script

1st Rumours of wars for Israel must complete to finish Matthew 24:6. The most likely way for this to be accomplished is an actual war between Israel and Iran, Hamas, and Hezbollah.

2nd (Added this chapter) A notable war (possibly Israel-Iran) that has associated with it some kind of wonders in the heavens. Exactly what these wonders are is not given.

3rd (Added this chapter) The sun shall turn into darkness and the moon into blood (possibly a time of notable solar eclipses and blood moons) before the great war that launches the day of the Lord.

4th Next, All nations initiate an agreement removing land from Israel in the name of Peace.

5th This initial Peace agreement by all nations does not have to be for seven years, or allow the temple to be erected or reveal the identity of the Antichrist ... yet.

1st Next, The day of the Lord launches with a great war sometime after that Peace agreement initiated by all nations.

2nd The great war between the nations that launches the day of the Lord comes with a thief in the night kind of surprise and includes great earthquakes, famines, pestilences, and thick darkness across the world, making it difficult at times to see the sun, moon, and stars.

3rd All nations are severely punished in the beginning of the day of the Lord. Israel is also punished for having agreed to the Peace covenant but only in measure.

4th The time frame wherein the Antichrist rises to power is the birth pangs beginning phase of the day of the Lord.

5th The Four Horsemen of the Apocalypse start riding during the birth pangs beginning phase of the day of the Lord.

Daniel's 70th Week Prophetic Time Frame:

1st Sometime after all nations initiate the Peace covenant, removing land from Israel the Antichrist will confirm it for a period of 7 years. This begins Daniel's 70th Week.

2nd The shift of world power to the Antichrist during the birth pangs phase is completed at the moment he is the one to confirm the covenant with many that all nations initiated. That moment launches his seven-year rule and the 70th week of Daniel.

3rd (Added this chapter) The Antichrist will have unprecedented influence over the Muslim masses in the world in order to be able to allow the Jews to rebuild their temple.

Western Nations Are Devastated

CHAPTER NINE

Isaiah & Zephaniah: Western Nations Hit Hardest

Covered in this Chapter: The United States and Western Europe will be hardest hit in the beginning phase (birth pangs) of *the day of the Lord.*

Covered in this Chapter: Foreigners will flee out of the United States and Western Europe in the beginning phase (birth pangs) of *the day of the Lord.*

The next witness to describe events during the beginning phase of *the day of the Lord* (end times) is the prophet Isaiah. Consider his words recorded in chapter 13, where he attaches the birth pangs term while discussing *the day of the Lord.* Although he does not allude to the *Peace* agreement here, his focus is on the impact against *all nations* during the beginning phase of *the day of the Lord.* What he has to say appears to be directed toward the Western powers and it is ominous.

> *The noise of a multitude in the mountains, like as of a great people; a tumultuous noise of the <u>kingdoms of nations gathered together</u>: the <u>LORD of hosts mustereth the host of the battle.</u> Isaiah 13:4*

Isaiah describes the scene of a great gathering together of many nations for battle. It is a large gathering like a *multitude in the mountains* and *a great people,* as well as *kingdoms and nations gathered together,* indicating a great multitude of nations. This is similar to Jesus' words in Matthew 24:7 where He said that *nation shall rise against nation and kingdom against kingdom* also covering the multitude of nations by using both the terms *nation* and *kingdom.* In line with Isaiah is Joel 3:2, where the Lord gathers *all nations and brings them down into the valley of Jehoshaphat* to be punished. Then Isaiah tells us what this punishment is.

> *They come from a far country, from the end of heaven, even the* L*ORD, and the weapons of his indignation, to destroy the whole land. ⁶Howl ye; for <u>the day of the</u>* L*<u>ORD</u> <u>is at hand; it</u> <u>shall come as a destruction from the Almighty</u>. Isaiah 13:5*

We are being told that this great gathering of nations and kingdoms is within *the day of the Lord.* We are also told *it shall come as destruction from the Almighty,* which like the *valley of Jehoshaphat* in Joel 3:2 is judgment against the nations.

> *And they shall be afraid: pangs and sorrows shall take hold of them; they shall be <u>in pang as a woman that travaileth</u>: they shall be amazed one at another; their faces shall be as flames. Isaiah 13:8*

After being told in verse 5 that the events being described are *the day of the Lord* (end times), we are now told they represent its beginning phase by the usage of a birth pangs phrase *as a woman that travaileth.* We have connected Matthew 24:7-8 also as birth pangs of *the day of the Lord* along with 1 Thessalonians 5:2-3 and Jeremiah 30. However, Isaiah appears to add new details relating to this developing picture. Consider verse 5 again but from another perspective.

> *<u>They come from a far country</u>, from the end of heaven, even the* L*ORD, and the <u>weapons of his indignation</u>, to destroy the whole land. ⁶Howl ye; for <u>the day of the</u>* L*<u>ORD</u> <u>is at hand; it</u> <u>shall come as a destruction from the Almighty</u>. Isaiah 13:5*

By reading this literally it would appear that from *a far country* come *the weapons of his indignation, to destroy the whole land* and this is in the beginning phase of *the day of the Lord* because a birth pangs term is present. Since the destruction comes from a country far away from those being destroyed, it could mean several things. It could mean weapons that travel great distances such as rockets sent from one country to another, bringing destruction with them. However, it could also mean individuals far from home who bring destruction to others. If this second example is the case, then it is describing the types of individuals from foreign lands that have entered their host countries (Western nations) to harm them like those who carried out the September 11, 2001 attacks. It is in verse 14 that clarity on this point is provided.

> *And it shall be as the chased roe, and as a sheep that no man taketh up: they shall every man turn to his own people, and flee every one into his own land. Isaiah 13:14*

Here we are told that every man shall *turn to his own people.* That speaks to foreigners returning to their land of origin. An example would be people who came from Middle Eastern countries and live in the United States and Europe. We are told such individuals will *flee every one into his own land.* When foreigners must *flee* out of countries back to their land of origin it indicates the welcome mat for them in those foreign lands has run out. When verses 5 and 14 are viewed together we see why this happens. Those who *come from a far country* are used as *weapons* of God's *indignation* and are no longer welcome in the foreign lands where they were living. The only option remaining for them is to *turn back to* [their] *own people, and flee every one into his own land.*

This fleeing *every one into his own land* indicates that during the beginning part of *the day of the Lord* (end times), a mass exodus of immigrants out from the lands they migrated to unfolds. Apparently the main reason rests on the fact that as the Scripture is telling us, some of those foreigners have been used as *weapons of his indignation.* As the nations reel in the agony and destruction that accompanies the start of *the day of the Lord,* apparently those native to the land recognize that foreigners were responsible for the destruction that unfolded. As a result, it becomes unsustainable for those foreigners to remain in their host countries and causes *every man turn to his own people, and flee every one into his own land.* And they do not casually leave those nations but they *flee,* which indicates the need to leave in a hurry. Such a description of foreigners needing to leave appears to indicate the impact that the beginning phase of *the day of the Lord* has on Western nations. And there is another Scripture that also alludes to the Western nations as being a major target for destruction during *the day of the Lord.*

CRITICAL CONCLUSION: FOREIGNERS FLEE WESTERN NATIONS IN THE BEGINNNG OF *THE DAY OF THE LORD*

Adding to the case that during *the day of the Lord* Western nations are the ones struck hardest is Scripture found in the Book of Zephaniah. In chapter 1 starting in verse 15 some specific details concerning *the day of the Lord* are given wherein we are told it will be a day of *wrath, trouble, distress, wasteness, desolation, darkness, gloominess and thick darkness.* Now consider the following details provided in verses 16 and 18.

16A day of the trumpet and alarm against the fenced cities, and against the high towers. Zephaniah 1:16

Verse 16 appears to be literally telling us that nations under the belief they are secure will be struck a terrible blow. They are nations that have *fenced cities,* which indicate notable protection. They also possess *high towers* along with those fences. Such towers are designed to provide a military intelligence advantage by allowing enemies to be seen from a distance. In other words, it appears that the nations being described here are the most prepared in terms of national defense. Now consider verse 18.

18Neither their silver nor gold shall be able to deliver them in the day of the Lord's wrath... Zephaniah 1:18

Zephaniah also informs us that these nations possessing strong military defenses also possess great wealth and find that neither their strong military nor great wealth does them any good during *the day of the Lord.* To impart this understanding, he employs terms universally understood as indicating great wealth ... *silver* and *gold.* But the real significance of what is being relayed here is his identification of wealthy and well defended nations as the ones being struck. They are the ones that have the *silver* and *gold* and powerful militaries yet discover that during *the day of the Lord* it cannot deliver them from that great day of *wrath.*

By Zephaniah identifying nations that have both great wealth as well as strong national defenses, we can now understand this to indicate what is referred to today as the Western powers. Considering that it is the Western powers who are the main movers within the United Nations, it will be they whom ultimately will provide the final OK for *all nations* to remove land from Israel in a *Peace* agreement. Without the Western powers moving against Israel such a move by the United Nations (*all nations*) could not go through. Therefore, it appears to be the "West" that Zephaniah identifies as being hit very hard during *the day of the Lord.*

It should be understood that nowhere within Zephaniah 1 is there any mention of birth pangs so the events being described here cannot be isolated to the beginning of the *day of the Lord*.

Prophetic Script

Pre-Birth Pangs Prophetic Time Frame:

1st Rumours of wars for Israel must complete to finish Matthew 24:6. The most likely way for this to be accomplished is an actual war between Israel and Iran, Hamas, and Hezbollah.

Warning # 1 ... Before the "End Times" Launch

2nd (Added this chapter) A notable war (possibly Israel-Iran) that has associated with it some kind of wonders in the heavens. Exactly what these wonders are is not given.

Warning # 2 ... Before the "End Times" Launch

3rd (Added this chapter) The sun shall turn into darkness and the moon into blood (possibly a time of notable solar eclipses and blood moons) before the great war that launches the day of the Lord.

Warning # 3 ... Before the "End Times" Launch

4th Next, All nations initiate an agreement removing land from Israel in the name of Peace.

5th This initial Peace agreement by all nations does not have to be for seven years, or allow the temple to be erected or reveal the identity of the Antichrist ... yet.

Birth Pangs Prophetic Time Frame:

1st Next, The day of the Lord launches with a great war sometime after that Peace agreement initiated by all nations.

2nd The great war between the nations that launches the day of the Lord comes with a thief in the night kind of surprise and includes great earthquakes, famines, pestilences, and thick darkness across the world, making it difficult at times to see the sun, moon, and stars.

3rd All nations are severely punished in the beginning of the day of the Lord. Israel is also punished for having agreed to the Peace covenant but only in measure.

4th The time frame wherein the Antichrist rises to power is the birth pangs beginning phase of the day of the Lord.

5th The Four-Horsemen of the Apocalypse start riding during the birth pangs beginning phase of the day of the Lord.

6th (Added this chapter) During the birth pangs beginning phase of the day of the Lord foreigners will flee the United States and Western Europe.

7th (Added this chapter) During the birth pangs beginning phase of the day of the Lord the United States and Western Europe are probably hit the hardest.

Daniel's 70th Week Prophetic Time Frame:

1st Sometime after all nations initiate the Peace covenant removing land from Israel, the Antichrist will confirm it for a period of seven-years. This begins Daniel's 70th Week.

2nd The shift of world power to the Antichrist during the birth pangs phase is completed at the moment he is the one to confirm the covenant with many that all nations initiated. That moment launches his seven-year rule and the 70th week of Daniel.

3rd The Antichrist will have unprecedented influence over the Muslim masses in the world in order to be able to allow the Jews to rebuild their temple.

CHAPTER TEN

Warning # 4 Luke: Mass Christian Persecution a Clear Pre-Birth Pangs Sign

Covered in this Chapter: During the time frame just before the launch of *the day of the Lord* there will be many deceptive Christian teachers and leaders not rightly dividing the word of God.

Covered in this Chapter: During the time frame just before the launch of *the day of the Lord* there will be a notable increase in the martyrdom of Christians.

We have covered a multitude of Scriptures, which all point toward the same chain of grand events occurring during the pre-birth pangs prophetic time frame which unfolds just before *the day of the Lord* launches. There will be a notable war (Israel-Iran?) (resolving *rumours of wars*) associated with some kind of *wonders in the heavens*. There will also be another celestial sign wherein the *sun shall be turned into darkness, and the moon into blood* before *the day of the Lord* begins. The final sign is a *Peace covenant* initiated by *all nations* that removes land from Israel. All of these events take place within the pre-birth pangs time frame just before the horrific *day of the Lord* starts and act as a warning of its approach. Without these signs unfolding *the day of the Lord* will not begin!

But there are two other pre-birth pang signs Jesus tells us will exist as general conditions before *the day of the Lord* begins and they specifically relate to Christians. He tells us both conditions must be in place during the time of the *wars and rumours of wars* and then when the *Peace* treaty by *all nations* unfolds. However, both of these additional signs are unpleasant for Christians to consider.

The first sign presented is found in Matthew chapter 24 and given just before Jesus tells us to look for *wars and rumours of wars*. The second sign comes from the

Book of Luke chapter 21, which represents another record of Jesus' words on the Mount of Olives, adding a detail not included in Mathew's account.

1ˢᵗ General Sign: They shall deceive many

In the next two verses Jesus is beginning His answer to the apostles' question relating to the signs leading up to the start of the end times. Their question is very specific: ... *what shall be the sign of thy coming, and of the end of the world.* In response Jesus begins with the following words.

---

⁴ And Jesus answered and said unto them, Take heed that no man deceive you. ⁵ For many shall come in my name, saying, I am Christ; and shall deceive many. Matthew 24:4-5

It is deception that comes to Jesus' mind first in describing the social conditions that will exist leading up to the beginning of *the day of the Lord.* He says *take heed that no man deceive you.* It is a very direct warning to the believer to be on guard for deception. And because it is first in His rendition of warnings, it is reasonable to conclude that deception will be a significant factor for Christians at the time just before the start of *the day of the Lord.* But that, of course, raises the most obvious question: Deception from whom? Who is it that the believer must exercise this great caution against lest they be deceived by them? In His next breath He appears to settle the issue.

For many shall come in my name, saying, I am Christ; and shall deceive many. (Matthew 24:5)

Many Christians believe that in this verse Jesus is saying many false Christs will appear before the end times begin. However, a closer look at the wording used in the verse opens up another possibility. That other possibility begins when Jesus tells us that these deceivers will *come in my name.* In other words, we are being told they will come in the name of Jesus. So in this opening phrase we see Jesus referring back to Himself by saying they will *come in my name* and this provides an important clue as to who it is that Jesus is warning about. This is because it is common knowledge that those who come in the name of Jesus are typically Christian leaders and ministers. Technically, each and every Christian minister preaches in the name of Jesus and not in their own name.

Next in the verse Jesus points out that the deceivers will be *saying, I am Christ,* a phrase that presents two distinct possibilities as to whom it is that is being referred to as Christ. Is Jesus telling us the deceivers are claiming to be Christ themselves or is He alerting us that they will be acknowledging that Jesus is Christ? At first glance it may appear He is saying that they will claim to be Christ. But since Jesus is speaking in the first person here, it is equally possible that He is once again referring back to Himself just as He did in the opening part of the verse. Since Christian leaders and ministers come in the name of Jesus, then the context established by that opening phrase would seem to make it more likely He is referring back to himself, again here indicating that those coming in His name will also acknowledge Him as the Christ. Here are some other points to consider.

If Jesus meant to indicate these deceivers would present themselves to be Christ, then it is unlikely He would have first indicated they would come in His name, a clear reference to teachers and followers of Christ. Also, if He wanted to indicate they would come in His name and yet claim to be Christ, wouldn't He have spoken a little differently, perhaps phrasing it something like, "saying <u>they</u> are Christ" instead of *saying I am Christ*? But there is another issue raised and it has to do with simple logic.

It should be noted that many Christs cannot deceive many people. That is because the term Christ is a one-of-a-kind reference. Whereas one claiming to be Christ might deceive many, each new claim of Christhood dilutes the impact of all others making a similar claim. Ultimately, if enough made the claim, it would diminish into derision and laughter with few being deceived. Essentially, one false christ may fool many people, or many false christs may fool a few people, but many false christs cannot fool many people. And Jesus is telling us that *many* will come in His name and *many* will be deceived. So based on that logic alone, it appears that Jesus in this verse is not yet referring to false christs. But consider now the wording He uses when He clearly does discuss false christs much later in Matthew.

"For false christs and false prophets will rise and show great signs and wonders to deceive, if possible, even the elect."
Matthew 24:24

This particular warning is set within *the day of the Lord* and not within the pre-birth pangs period of verse 5. In this verse some are actually claiming to be Christ, even showing *great signs and wonders.* Notice the different wording here from that in verse 5. In verse 24 it is made clear that they are *false christs and false prophets,* whereas in verse 5 there is no such indication. In verse 5 it is indicated that they will *come in my name,* but in verse 24 there is no such indication. Therefore, for the reasons presented here, it appears more reasonable to conclude that verse 5 is discussing Christian leaders deceiving *many* people and that *false christs* are addressed later in verse 24.

This, therefore, is the first general sign Jesus provides just before the launch of *the day of the Lord.* But we are also told there will be *many* of them whom will deceive *many.* This word *many* indicates that these Christian leaders will have access to the ears of a multitude of Christians.

2ⁿᵈ General Sign: Significant Persecution of Christians

Chapter 21 in the Book of Luke begins with essentially the same litany of events as we see in Matthew chapter 24. It too is a record of the rendition delivered by Jesus on the Mount of Olives. But it adds a detail that was not included in Matthew's account---the persecution of Christians. Immediately after describing the beginning events He informs us that ...*before all these, they shall lay their hands on you, and persecute you, delivering you up to the synagogues, and into prisons, being brought before kings and rulers for my name's sake (Luke 21:12).* Since He tells us that this will happen *before* the beginning of the end times, we now know that notable Christian persecution will occur in the pre-birth pangs prophetic time frame and will be one of the general signs to look for. Now consider the details of this verse in the original Greek.

The phrase *they shall lay their hands on you* in the original Greek is *epiballō,* which means "seizing one to lead him off as a prisoner." They will *persecute diōkō* "to make to run or flee, put to flight, drive away." But if they do not run or flee then *delivering you paradidōmi* "to be judged, condemned, punished, scourged, tormented, put to death." Who does it ... the *synagogues synagōgē* "an assembly of men." In plain English it is saying this.

"An assembly of men will put to flight and drive away Christians. Those that are caught will be seized as prisoners and led away to be judged, condemned, tormented and put to death."

If this rendition sounds familiar it should. It has been unfolding on a massive scale across the Middle East and Africa with the horrific persecution of Christians since the year 2003. Consider what Christians in Iraq have been facing at the hands of the terrorist organization ISIS. It is mass expulsions from their homes and those unable to escape face judgments resulting in the removal of their heads. That includes the children as well. Within the nation of Iraq, out of 1,400,000 Christians living peacefully there in 2003, only 400,000 remained by 2014! That means over 1,000,000 have been driven away from their homes. What a great persecution, and that is only in the nation of Iraq.

However, ISIS is only the most recognized terrorist organization doing these atrocities. Their notoriety went global due to the death of some reporters at their hands. After certain reporters were killed, the media began following the carnage with zeal ... not before. In Africa, Boko Haram, the terrorist organization attempting to establish a Muslim Caliphate there, has also been methodically cleansing entire regions of Christians through flight and murder.

The persecution of Christians today has now reached a scale that has not been seen in centuries, fulfilling the second pre-birth pangs sign Jesus warned of. It should be noted that this great persecution is occurring during the same time in which many deceptive Christian leaders have risen up deceiving many, primarily through the omission of the full Gospel.

Prophetic Script

Pre-Birth Pangs Prophetic Time Frame:

1st Rumours of wars for Israel must complete to finish Matthew 24:6. The most likely way for this to be accomplished is an actual war between Israel and Iran, Hamas, and Hezbollah.

Warning # 1 ... Before the "End Times" Launch

2nd (Added this chapter) A notable war (possibly Israel-Iran) that has associated with it some kind of wonders in the heavens. Exactly what these wonders are is not given.

Warning # 2 ... Before the "End Times" Launch

3rd (Added this chapter) The sun shall turn into darkness and the moon into blood (possibly a time of notable solar eclipses and blood moons) before the great war that launches the day of the Lord.

Warning # 3 ... Before the "End Times" Launch

4th Next, All nations initiate an agreement removing land from Israel in the name of Peace.

5th This initial Peace agreement by all nations does not have to be for seven years, or allow the temple to be erected or reveal the identity of the Antichrist ... yet.

6th (Added this chapter) During the time frame just before the launch of the day of the Lord there will be many deceptive Christian teachers and leaders not rightly dividing the word of God.

7th (Added this chapter) During the time frame just before the launch of the day of the Lord there will be a notable increase in the martyrdom of Christians.

Birth Pangs Prophetic Time Frame:

1st Next, The day of the Lord launches with a great war sometime after that Peace agreement initiated by all nations.

2nd The great war between the nations that launches the day of the Lord comes with a thief in the night kind of surprise and includes great earthquakes, famines, pestilences, and thick darkness across the world, making it difficult at times to see the sun, moon, and stars.

3rd All nations are severely punished in the beginning of the day of the Lord. Israel is also punished for having agreed to the Peace covenant but only in measure.

4th The time frame wherein the Antichrist rises to power is the birth pangs beginning phase of the day of the Lord.

5th The Four Horsemen of the Apocalypse start riding during the birth pangs beginning phase of the day of the Lord.

6th During the birth pangs beginning phase of the day of the Lord, foreigners will flee the United States and Western Europe.

7th During the birth pangs beginning phase of the day of the Lord, the United States and Western Europe are probably hit the hardest.

Daniel's 70th Week Prophetic Time Frame:

1st Sometime after all nations initiate the Peace covenant removing land from Israel the Antichrist will confirm it for a period of seven years. This begins Daniel's 70th Week.

2nd The shift of world power to the Antichrist during the birth pangs phase is completed at the moment he is the one to confirm the covenant with many that all nations initiated. That moment launches his 7 year rule and the 70th week of Daniel.

3rd The Antichrist will have unprecedented influence over the Muslim masses in the world in order to be able to allow the Jews to rebuild their temple.

Summation

The Scriptural flow of events:

1. **War Resolving Notable Rumours of Wars for Israel and Wonders In the Heavens:** Israel's involvement in a notable war most likely involving the nation of Iran. Associated with that war should be some kind of *wonders in the heavens* either just before or during that war, allowing it to be clearly identified as completing two specific verses of Scripture.

2. **The sun shall be darkened and the moon turned into blood:** Exactly what this sign is we cannot be certain. But it will take place before *the day of the Lord* begins.

3. **Great Christian Persecution:** Before the day of the Lord launches there will be a notable persecution of Christians taking place.

4. **A U.N. Initiated Middle East Peace Agreement:** Following that notable war and its heavenly wonders, the flow of events turns to a major peace agreement removing some land from Israel. This agreement will, in some manner, involve *all nations.*

5. **The Great War:** It is after that peace agreement removing some land from Israel and initiated by *all nations* (United Nations) that launches mankind's most horrific war, marking the start of the birth pangs beginning phase of *the day of the Lord.* Accompanying that great war will be great earthquakes, famines, and pestilences across the globe.

6. **The Antichrist and the Holy Temple:** After the birth pangs beginning phase of *the day of the Lord* the world power structure is completely altered. No longer is it *all nations* that is significant but a new Middle Eastern leader who gains great power by *conquering and to conquer* during those birth pangs. So significant is this transition of power that it is he alone who is needed to confirm the agreement previously initiated by *all nations* for a period of seven years. It is at that point in time when he allows the Jews to rebuild their holy temple on the Temple Mount.

This thesis is presented as a sincere representation of what this author believes the multitude of Scripture covered herein is saying. It is recognized that some of it runs hard against traditional teachings on this subject. But it should also be recognized that many of those traditional teachings are often confusing and contradictory.

Only time will tell if what is presented here is a correct reading of Scripture.

May you accept Jesus Christ as your one and only Savior.

David

www.ingramcontent.com/pod-product-compliance
Lightning Source LLC
Chambersburg PA
CBHW071640050426
42443CB00026B/776